Stuck in My Head

an offbeat look
at music and mental health

2nd Edition

by Michael Dane

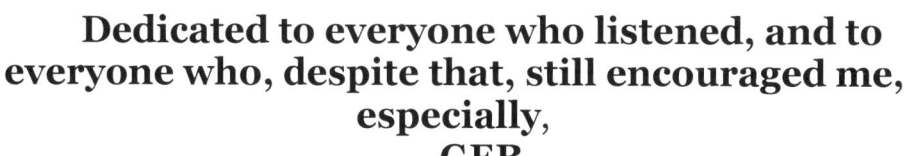

Dedicated to everyone who listened, and to everyone who, despite that, still encouraged me, especially,
GEB

CONTENTS

CONVERSATIONS

"If you pour some music on whatever's wrong,
it'll sure help."

--Levon Helm

Common Ground

If you're like me, you're a middle-aged Jewish man with an irritated prostate and a history of panic attacks. That would be a weird coincidence, so let's say, for the sake of argument, you're not *exactly* like me.

You probably didn't go through high school carrying a briefcase and a clarinet. *You* might not have been a cybernetics major in college, and *you* probably didn't drop out of college after three years to join the Air Force. Or get discharged from the Air Force after six weeks for what might be called 'emotional reasons.'

Most likely, *you've* never sung "Ave Maria" at a Hindu funeral, or, for that matter, done standup comedy in the middle of a frozen lake. Maybe *you* haven't lived in a dozen different cities, or changed your religion. Twice.

So, in the details, your life may have played out a bit differently than mine. There is something you and I have in common, though.

We will all, at some point, go out of our minds. You could be completely out of yours while you're reading this. I'm not judging here.

I've been out of *my* mind, or at least out of my 'right' mind, more than a few times, and during most of those times, music has helped me get my mind right again.

I've also had good friends and plenty of therapy. But when I start to veer off the rails, if my friends are busy and my therapist is booked, my first instinct is to turn on some music.

In a curious quirk of the English language, being 'out of your mind' is negative, but getting 'out of your head' is healthy. In fact, if you get stuck *in* your head for too long, you'll probably end up going 'out of your mind.'

I'll leave those distinctions to the professionals. What I know is that music helps in either case. When the voices in my head start to form an improv troupe, music keeps the scene together.

Likewise, If I get stuck on some unhealthy thought, and I focus on the right music for a few minutes, I end up slightly less stuck.

To this end, I've been putting together music mixes since the days when you had to point your cassette recorder at the radio, and hope that the DJ wouldn't talk over the end of your song before you hit 'stop.' Before there were 'curated playlists,' we had to do our own damned 'curation'—imagine that, kids!

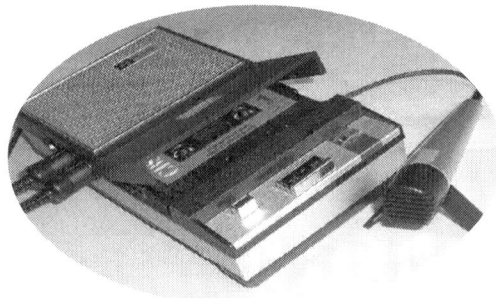

At one point, I had nearly a thousand mix tapes. There were songs recorded off the radio, and songs from albums I borrowed from friends. I became a musical hoarder.

I got to a point where I could tell, simply by looking at a cassette, exactly how much room was left for that one last song to make the mix perfect.

I'm not talking about the cliché 'mix-tape' you throw together to win back an ex-girlfriend. I've made morning mixes, angry mixes, meditation mixes, and travelling mixes. Most of them, however 'perfect' they were, were only heard by me.

Of course, now that every note of music ever performed can be accessed with a few clicks, I can put together something to fit every possible emotional state—a backdrop for every mood swing. Low-grade anxiety, with mild depression? Sure, I can score that.

If I'm feeling particularly scattered, I might put on a Mozart string quartet. The mathematical precision of the notes, the reassuring structure and form—those are things I can grab and hold, until I get back on track, brain-wise.

If I'm feeling too jangly, I might look for serenity, seventeenth-century style, by wrapping myself in a Bach chorale. Give me twelve minutes with Gregorio Allegri, and I might be able to drown out some seriously unproductive random noise.

But don't think that I only escape with the music of white guys who died hundreds of years ago. There are times when my trip back to sanity absolutely must include some Nina Simone. For instance, those days when I feel like going to a protest march at a church in a blues club.

Sometimes I might completely disappear into some late eighties Prince. Because, and I quote, *"If you ain't hip to the rare house quake—shut up, already—damn!"*

Other times, I can get so lost in a Miles Davis solo that I need a GPS unit to find my way back to whatever was bothering me in the first place.

Just between us, there are also times when the only music that gets my head straight is decidedly middle-of-the-road—the sonic equivalent of Kraft macaroni and cheese.

Are there times when I *need* to hear The Eagles' *Greatest Hits*? Yes. Do I hate myself a little for it? Sure.

Whatever the soundtrack, when I choose 'music for self-medication' (which would be a great album title), I listen differently. The music enters my ears the same way, but once it gets to my brain, I like to engage in something I call Really Listening™.

Okay, so it's not actually a trademarked thing. But it is different than the listening we usually do. In a culture where news broadcasts have theme songs and streaming services have playlists curated specifically for vacuuming, music is literally everywhere.

~turally, if it's everywhere, it might as well be nowhere *~orry to drop some Zen on you without warning)*. For many people, music is *only* 'background.' It's audio wallpaper, and, frankly, wallpaper has never really helped me feel better.

For music to be at all therapeutic, I need to treat the notes and chords like they're landmarks on a trail map, showing me a way to get from the mental wilderness back to Camp Sanity.

It's about telling my neurons to disconnect from whatever is causing the crazy at that moment, and latch onto the melody like it's a zip line.

This is why, when I set up the speakers at my desk (where I spend most of my day), they need to be as far apart as the cords can reach, and angled so they point directly at me from each side. That's because I want to connect with my music *viscerally*.

I used to use a Bluetooth speaker. It was this very sleek, minimalist, black cuboid gizmo that worked magically, and without wires. A couple of clicks and there was my music, coming straight at me out of said space-age gizmo. Which was the problem.

The deal is, if I'm listening to Loggins and Messina, I want one of them on my left and one on my right—they should *not* sound like they're standing next to each other.

The same theory applies to Seals and Crofts, and while we're at it, I'd prefer that Crosby and Stills come out of a different speaker than Nash and Young.

RCA released a series of albums under the 'Living Stereo' moniker, and for a few years, everybody was making sounds go from one ear to the other. It was like the beginning of the Technicolor era, when every studio went all in on the new technology, and the movies looked almost *too* colorful.

Stereo separation was a huge advance in recording technology. For one thing, wthout it, there would have been no 'progressive rock.'

With sound separation (especially if you're listening through headphones) the Rush album *2112* is mind-blowing, man. Without it, you're just listening to a guy screeching about priests and temples.

Getting back to my speakers (in case you thought I'd forgotten my point), I'm finicky about them because I want music to be more than something I *hear*—I want it to be someplace I *go*.

If I'm listening to music because I need a kick in the ass, then I want to *feel* the kick in my ass. If I'm listening to music because I need comfort, then I want to feel like I'm wearing that music.

If I'm awake, there is probably music playing. If I'm asleep, I probably got there with music. As I write this sentence, I'm listening to my own "Music for Writing" mix--some solo cello, a few minutes of Samuel Barber, a bit of Brian Eno.

Naturally, *this* sentence was actually written about half an hour after the last one, because I got distracted by the music.

With mental illness, sometimes distraction is the entire point. My mind has a fun habit of latching on to a particularly unhealthy thought and magnifying it until that one thought takes up my entire skull.

Unless I play some music to point my focus toward something else, I could conceivably be stuck on that one toxic thought *for days*.

For most of my 'issues,' music has proven to be at least as helpful as therapy, with much less paperwork. The exception would be my OCD, since my music obsession probably *feeds* that. On the other hand, those playlists won't just alphabetize themselves.

As much as I try to surround myself with music, there are times when I am forced to take out my earbuds and interact with other human beings.

Luckily, I realized something recently that allowed me to finally get *comfortable* with my own mental quirks. I realized that I'm not walking down Crazy Boulevard alone.

According to a recent study, over forty-five million Americans have a mental illness. While that still leaves us with two hundred sixty some-odd million people who *don't*, it *is* more than ten percent of the population.

Even at ten percent, I'm convinced that estimate is on the low side. Just in my circle of friends, we've got: bipolar disorder, anxiety disorder, PTSD, depression, OCD, emotional withdrawal, and anti-social behavior.

My point is that, in my experience, mental illness is pretty normal. But I'd take it a step further. I would suggest that, on some level, *everybody* is crazy. We're all just listening to different songs.

I noticed a long time ago that I'm not wired like 'most people.' Only recently did I figure out that most people aren't wired like 'most people.' As soon as I figured out that *nobody* is normal, I started to cut myself slack for my own lunacy.

In turn, this led me to develop a comprehensive, unifying theory of psychological behavior, based on years of anecdotal research. I believe there are only *two* mental states, encompassing all observable aspects of human behavior—there's good crazy, and there's bad crazy.

For example, most of us at some point have collected something—coins, baseball cards, Grateful Dead concert bootlegs . . . If you collect anything, there's *some* crazy involved. The very concept behind 'collecting' is crazy—"I have this one thing that I think is cool, and now I need to get as many things like that as I can find!"

As far as I'm concerned, if you buy one refrigerator magnet on your trip to Key West, nobody would call you crazy. If you pay forty bucks on eBay because you need 'Rhode Island' to give you all fifty states, you're *kinda* crazy.

It's really a question of *what* you collect. If you have hundreds of refrigerator magnets, that's 'good crazy.' If you're collecting Nazi memorabilia, or human skulls, that's probably 'bad crazy.'

Out of all the many psychological and psychiatric remedies available, music is the most reliable. It can bring you back if you lose your moorings, take you away if you need to escape, and make the ride smoother when you hit some potholes.

We live in a perpetually medicated society where most people want nothing more than to *stop* feeling. So, they queue up for the latest pill that can mute their craziness and allow them to be functional cogs again.

Of course, this is despite *"side effects which may include nausea, blindness, rash, ulcers, liver failure, and thoughts of suicide."* At least you're not depressed anymore.

On the other hand, if you medicate with music—if you're Really Listening™--you might get past that rough stretch, and there's *zero* risk of side effects!

Actually, there is one possible side effect. You *could* end up with a song stuck in your head, but that feeling usually goes away when you play another song.

Sometimes, when I'm losing it (even if I don't know what 'it' is), instead of trying to escape, I'll double down. Sometimes, I need to hear about *other* people's crazy before I can be ready to face my own. In that spirit, what follows is a mix of songs about cracking up, breaking down, and flipping out.

"Angie Baby," Helen Reddy, 1974

As a teenager, I didn't listen to anything too challenging. Mostly, it was Top 40 AM radio. Still, amidst all the sappy pop, there was this song, and it was the first time I'd ever heard a song about a crazy person.

The lyric is a bit cryptic but from what I can tell, Angie lived through her radio, and forced this voyeur (stalker) to live in her radio as her slave. Or she killed him. *"She's a little touched, you know."*

"Brain Cloudy Blues," Bob Wills, 1946

The leading cause of mental illness, at least according to male songwriters, is women. Although most of the lyric is typical 'you done me wrong' material, the line *"my brain is cloudy and my soul is upside down"* kills me.

Also, I love 'western swing' music, which sounds like some jazz musicians got lost going to a gig, and were forced to do a show behind a barn.

"I've Always Been Crazy," Waylon Jennings, 1978

"I've always been crazy, but it's kept me from going insane." A groundbreaking psychological study in which Dr. Jennings suggests that being crazy may, in fact, prevent mental illness.

His theory was roundly discredited at the time, and he soon abandoned his promising psychiatric career to focus on creating a theme song for "The Dukes of Hazard."

"People Are Strange," The Doors, 1967

Think of this track as a musical intake form. Be sure to check all the boxes that apply: delusions, hallucinations, loneliness, feelings of isolation . . .

Special recognition to the winner of the Tautology in Rock award, Jim Morrison. Yes, Jim, *"people ARE strange, when you're a stranger."*

"I'm Going Slightly Mad," Queen, 1991

This is probably where most of us are on the spectrum of mental illness— *"slightly mad."* The lyric here serves as an excellent diagnostic test.

If you think you see *"a thousand and one daffodils begin to dance in front of you,"* or have ever said, *"I think I'm a banana tree,"* you should probably contact a professional. In any case, *"one wave short of a shipwreck"* is a great description of being crazy.

"Maxwell's Silver Hammer," The Beatles, 1969

The same guy who wrote 'Wonderful Christmastime' came up with this disturbing ditty about a sociopathic serial killer. It's like an episode of Dexter, directed by Wes Anderson and scored by Baz Luhrmann.

Savvy listeners will notice Ringo's virtuoso anvil playing. Oh, and in case you're not sure, Maxwell would be an example of 'bad crazy.'

"Manic Depression," Jimi Hendrix, 1967

Of course, if this song had been written today, it would have been called "Bipolar Disorder," which doesn't rock quite as hard.

Not technically about mental illness in a clinical sense, though any qualified shrink would agree that *"manic depression is a frustrating mess."*

"Paranoid," Black Sabbath, 1970

"People think I'm insane because I am frowning all the time." Well, Ozzie, admittedly the frowning doesn't help, but people might also be referring to the time you urinated on a tomb across from the Alamo.

Or the time you goose-stepped on top of a record executives desk (and <u>then</u> urinated in his wine glass), or the time you bit the head off a dove, or the time you bit the head off a bat. But, you're right, Ozzy—it's probably the frowning.

"I Wanna Be Sedated," The Ramones, 1978

There are rules that say you can't get prescription narcotics just because you *'wanna be sedated.'* Apparently, you have to go through all these hoops with some sort of doctor.

By the way, you could also go with their earlier song, "Gimme Gimme Shock Treatment," because, when dealing with mental illness, it's important to consider multiple protocols.

"Basket Case," Green Day, 1994

Panic disorder with a killer drum part, this is what my anxiety would sound like if it played guitar and wore eyeliner. *"Am I just paranoid, or am I just stoned?"* Well, Billie Joe, in my experience, those two are NOT mutually exclusive.

"Brain Damage," Pink Floyd, 1973

This one is perfect for those days we all have now and then. You know, those days when a co-worker asks you what's going on and you want to say, "Oh, nothing . . . '*heads exploding, dark foreboding*' . . . the usual."

"Crazy," Seal, 1991

Somehow, Seal makes "*crazy yellow people walking through (his) head*"—and the fact that "*one of them's got a gun*" --sound incredibly sexy. "*We're never gonna survive unless we get a little crazy.*" So, in a way, mental illness is actually *necessary*.

"Virtual Insanity," Jamiroquai, 1997

Forget the goofy Dr. Seuss hat and the trippy video . . . "*It's a wonder man can eat at all, when things are big that should be small.*" Sometimes, when your world is turned upside down, the best therapy is to get into a slowly rotating room and dance.

"Let's Go Crazy," Prince, 1984

In which Mr. Nelson suggests that we "look for the purple banana till they put us in the truck."

To review: if you think you're a banana tree, that's not good. But if you're looking for a purple banana, that's fine. At least until they put you in 'the truck.'

Amateur Hour

For almost every genre of music, I can think of a time when that music was *exactly* what I needed. Naturally, I file music into two categories; good and bad.

I'm not an opera buff, but there are times when I simply need to hear "*Nessun dorma.*" I'm not a huge country fan, but once in a while, I need to hear some Merle Haggard.

In fact, there are only a handful of musical styles that I avoid. I don't listen to a lot of Mongolian throat singing, but that's only because I can't sing along with it, and it makes my throat feel weird when I hear it.

I've never really embraced Celtic music, which, from what I can tell, is the same jig, or maybe it's a sea shanty, played at different speeds.

I'm not wild about 'death metal,' which, from what I can tell, is basically speed metal, only 'deathier.' The website *metalsucks.net* had this to say about a recent album—a feel-good collection called 'Necrotic Manifesto':

> *"A tech-death distillery . . . they ratchet up the early creepiness with horror-chic, and . . . hyper-rhythmic mortar bursts . . ."*

> I'm only speaking for myself here, but I can't imagine being in a headspace where tech-death, horror-chic mortar bursts would help.

Lastly, I believe I can say with some certainty that bagpipe music is horrible. Unless you're a dead Scotsman or in a Wings cover band playing "Mull of Kintyre," nobody enjoys bagpipe music.

Bagpipe *players* probably hate the sound of bagpipes even more than the rest of us, since they actually are closer to the thing *making* the godawful sound.

I have never met a bagpipe player, but I *have* talked with accordionists, didgeridoo enthusiasts, hip-hop harpists, and the occasional piano tuner. I played clarinet for a few years, I've sung a bit, sometimes in public, and not always well.

Still, I don't consider myself a musician. I have been *around* music for most of my life, though. I am what you might call a dedicated dabbler. The most profound difference between music and other human pursuits is that, in music, 'dabbling' is encouraged.

You wouldn't want your doctor to say, "I've recently started to dabble in open heart surgery," or your public defender to announce that he's just 'dabbling' in law. Music, however, welcomes dabblers.

I sometimes wish I had become a 'real' musician, but there's an upside to my amateur status. Since I don't have to struggle to make a living as a musician, I can truly *enjoy* music, while I struggle to make a living as a writer.

A surprising number of famous people were musical dabblers. When Einstein was asked how he conceived his relativity theory, he said it *"occurred to me by intuition, and music is the driving force behind this intuition."*

I often wonder how different the course of history would have been if certain people had decided to chase their musical dreams. Maybe Richard Nixon wouldn't have morphed into 'Tricky Dick" if he had simply focused on his piano playing.

Imagine Ben Franklin, who was an avid guitarist and violinist, hanging out in the 18th century indie alehouse scene. He'd be waiting to go on stage at open mics, playing gigs for free mead.

Although, if Ben had spent more time on music, the world might have had to wait for bifocals, or kites, or lightning. Whatever it was that he invented.

Most people, at some point in their lives, wonder what it would be like to be a musician. Whether you're singing into your hairbrush or shredding an air guitar solo, you've had a moment when you imagined yourself doing it *for real*.

Music is one of the few careers that inspire jealousy in people with . . . any other jobs. You don't hear people saying, "If I had to do it all over again, I'd pursue my passion for retail sales." Or, "I met an electrician at a party—THAT must be a fun way to make a living.

Music is different. When I worked the road, I usually hung out with musicians. They traveled the same territory, did the same types of gigs.

I preferred musicians to my fellow comics, since most comedians by nature were arrogant, neurotic, and needy. I already had that covered.

The musicians I met would bitch about the grind of having to play cover versions of Doobie Brothers songs for apathetic drunks in Ramada Inn lounges; of course, I was thinking, "Sign me up for that!" It sounded better than yelling one-liners about current events at hostile drunks in Ramada Inn lounges.

Besides, if you're grinding through thankless road gigs as a musician, you're still *getting paid for playing music*. If part of your *job* involves deciding when to sing "China Grove," you really don't have a bad job at all.

The path to a music career can involve years of study, great sacrifices, and slavish commitment to an artistic vision. Although, if I decided to become a musician today, I would have another option, one that wasn't available when I was younger.

I could bypass all the tedious suffering artist steps and just go to Craigslist. Any site where you can sell your car, rent an apartment, and connect with someone you saw on a train once, is sure to have something for aspiring musical talents.

These headlines from actual Craigslist ads should give you an idea of the wide range of opportunities available—

Looking to create an amazing time-altering superband

I'm sure this band would be *amazing*, but I think someone with 'time-altering' skills might want to do something more *significant* with their superpower than start a band.

Affordable Background Jazz

This ad might not attract many musicians with artistic integrity, but if a group actually *named* themselves 'Affordable Background Jazz,' they would be huge on the company holiday party circuit.

If you read past the headlines on Craigslist, you'll see heartwarming stories of artistic yearning and dedication--

Tuba Player for Hirc

Twenty-five years experience playing tuba. Experience with polka and miscellaneous dance music. Available most evenings and weekends. No drug or booze issues.

I'm pretty sure that by 'miscellaneous dance music' this guy means 'different kinds of polka.' And of course you're available evenings and weekends—you play the tuba--your schedule has been free for twenty-five years.

My favorite part is 'no drug issues.' Because there is nothing worse than a tuba player tripping balls.

White girl keyboardist in soul band needs lessons

I'm a nice white girl from the suburbs, classically trained in piano. Now I'm in a soul band, and I need help getting my groove on.

'*Now* I'm in a soul band' makes it look like she just *happened* to see a concert flyer in a bar, and suddenly realized she had this gig, or maybe she's being held *hostage* by a soul band, and they are now demanding that she get her groove on.

Tired of serious musicians?

You know those bands that suck so bad it's just amazing? That's what I am looking for. Can't sing, only know a few chords, used to play a Casio keyboard. We will play underground el-stops, and some easy to obtain gigs.

And here I would have thought that the 'underground el stop' circuit would already be booked solid, especially for bands who can't sing and hardly play.

Looking for a lyricist

I write music, but am having a difficult time trying to write a song about my life. I was born with a heart defect and had it fixed, only to have it come back.

Our doctor said that it was normal. However, I have Heart Failure. So I would like to write a song with lyrics describing my false trust in this doctor.

This just illustrates that there's a fine line between networking and oversharing.

You may not want to be on stage, or be able to come up with the right lyrics to describe medical malpractice, but you can still be in the music business. There's always the exciting field of djembe repair.

Repair my djembe

Years ago, I lent my djembe to a friend who had never heard that you should remove your rings before playing a djembe. Hopefully, I can find someone who can lace a new goatskin head onto it.

Those qualifications seem easy enough—you need to know what a djembe is (a handheld, skin-covered West African drum), and you need to have access to goatskin. Luckily, Craigslist can help you with the goat part, but you would have to skin it yourself.

What if you want to surround yourself with music, don't have what it takes to be on stage, and don't know your way around a djembe? There is one more path toward a career in music, and it also involves Craigslist.

You can open a piano store! First, rent a gigantic warehouse. Then, find a huge truck.

Then, check out the Craigslist 'free' category for any major city, and you'll find literally *dozens* of free pianos and organs. Because, while many people want to learn to play piano, and plenty of people own pianos, *nobody* wants to move one.

A Head Full of Music

My musical dabbling has never paid the bills, but my head has been filled with music for as long as I can remember. Actually, since before I can remember.

My mother enjoyed telling the story of when I was very young, and she was a single parent busting her ass as a nurse. She had to bring me to work with her, so I needed to entertain myself.

To hear her tell it, I would, for no apparent reason, take my pants off and run through the hallways, until she would find me and reunite me with my pants.

At which point, I would immediately take them off again and run through the hallways. This has nothing to do with music, but it is a cute story.

When I wasn't running half-naked through the hospital, I'm told that I played a ukulele. One of the patients, obviously sensing my innate musical gifts, gave me a plastic toy version, and I frequently 'performed' in patients' rooms. I'm guessing it wasn't always at the patient's request.

I wasn't raised in a musical home. Neither of my parents played an instrument or sang around the house. We did have a stereo, this massive thing the length of a living room wall. It played records on occasion, but mostly served as a flat surface for setting up the manger scene at Christmas.

The only albums I remember that we owned were fairly bland. We had Ferde Grofé's *Grand Canyon Suite* performed by the Philadelphia Orchestra. Imagine the classical music equivalent of smooth jazz—pleasant enough, but too safe, and dripping with musical clichés. Part of it sounded like the background music for an episode of *Bonanza*.

After re-listening to the thirty-some-odd minutes recently, for the first time in forty years, I was able to see its charms. Sure, there are hundreds of measures that sound like they're from a Disney movie about horses.

Still, the fact that, within the first ten minutes, I was transported back forty years to our living room in Lancaster, California makes it pretty good music.

My parents also had a few albums by a 'light classical' group called '101 Strings,' known for taking popular songs and removing the lyrics, the syncopation, the beat, and anything else that made the songs popular in the first place.

Even in my pre-teen years, I thought that the 101 Strings Orchestra was, in the language of my peers, lame. It always made me think of a hospital waiting room. Incredibly, these hundred and one musicians (*actually, a hundred and twenty-four*) sold fifty million records over a ten-year span.

I don't know what kind of music my father was into; we never talked about it. That's because he split when I was two years old. It's cool, though, because Elmer, the man who took on the *role* of 'Dad,' was great. I don't use the term stepdad. I prefer to think of him in baseball terms, as my 'relief Dad,' coming in during a tough spot to earn the save.

I know Elmer liked the crooners—Perry Como, Bing Crosby—but his favorite singer was Tennessee Ernie Ford. Ford's biggest hit was "Sixteen Tons," a jolly tune about working yourself to death as an indentured servant in a coal mine.

I don't remember ever seeing Elmer put a record on the turntable, and we certainly didn't share any musical memories, but he was more responsible than anyone for my love of music.

He was the one who encouraged me when I decided to join the junior high school band. He was the one who drove us to the music store to rent a clarinet for ten bucks a month. He took me back to get sheet music.

I generally picked out songs to play that I knew my parents enjoyed. I suppose I felt that, if they're paying for me to squeak and squawk while I try to learn this thing, the least I could do is squeak and squawk my way through some of *their* songs.

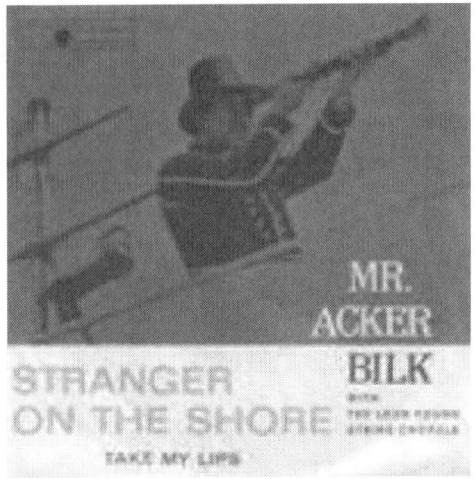

One of those songs was called "Stranger on the Shore," by Mr. Acker Bilk. I'm not calling him 'mister' for comic effect. He actually was *billed* as 'Mr. Acker Bilk.'

And in a pre-Beatles World, "Stranger" was the number one selling single in the U.K. in 1962. For some reason, radio wasn't interested in the b-side. "Take My Lips."

The other thing to Elmer's credit, musically, was that he tolerated my attempts to play these songs. I ended up fairly proficient at the clarinet, but when I started, there were a lot of unpleasant sounds.

It would have been more musical for me to use the clarinet as a drumstick and bang on something because blowing into it wasn't making anyone happy.

Of course, Mom had to endure the same sounds when I practiced, *and* sit through every school band concert, but she seemed less bothered by the noise, or at least better at blocking it out.

Gloria, as I could never *imagine* calling her, enjoyed listening to the radio, so she was aware of the 'pop' music of the day, but the singers she liked most were old-fashioned and smooth-voiced. She especially liked Eddy Arnold, who became known for a sound called 'countrypolitan.'

What is countrypolitan music? Imagine country music, but instead of a simple guitar, it's backed by *at least* a hundred and one strings, and you get the idea.

It's country music dressed for church in an ill-fitting suit. Anyway, I'm not sure how a blue-collar woman from Queens became a fan of 'The Tennessee Plowboy,' but he surely sang pretty.

Her favorite song was "Somewhere, My Love," which was Lara's theme from *Dr. Zhivago*. In fact, the first Christmas gift that I bought for her was a music box that played "Lara's Theme." Elmer gave me the money, but I chose it and paid for it, and I felt grown up for the first time.

The hit version of "Somewhere, My Love" was recorded by Andy Williams. He was Mom's musical crush. It's safe to say that, growing up, I heard more music by Andy Williams than any kids my age who weren't related to Andy Williams.

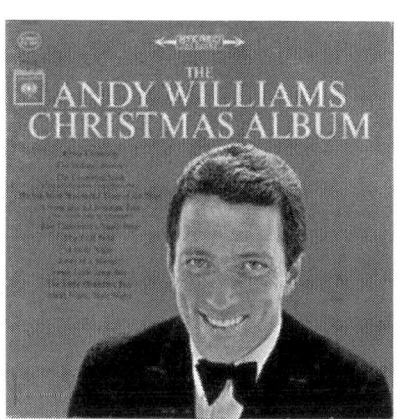

Beyond his popular 'Hit Parade' songs, Andy Williams provided the soundtrack to every Christmas I remember. "O Holy Night" may have been written in 1847, but to, me, it'll always be an Andy Williams song.

I may have left my vaguely Christian upbringing, but every year, when I hear "O Holy Night," I hear Andy Williams, and I get to see Mom again.

The first time I remember sharing music with my mother was when I was eight years old. I don't remember my mom ever discussing the news of the day, but on a Saturday morning in June, 1968, I could tell she was shaken, and I knew something important had happened.

For some historical context, in the five years between my third and eighth birthdays, two Kennedys were assassinated. I didn't look at it that way, I just knew it was a big deal.

We sat at the kitchen table around seven in the morning, earlier than I was used to as an eight-year old, and she tuned the radio to RFK's memorial service.

The service ended with Andy Williams' rendition of "The Battle Hymn of the Republic." I don't recall any words that were spoken between us, just a feeling of wanting my mom to stop crying.

It was the first time that I understood how one song could have such an impact, and on a very simplistic level, I got that it somehow made my mother feel better.

By the time I was eleven, I had a chance to assert my musical independence with my first record purchase. Here was a chance to show my parents that I was a rebel.

I could get something *really* out there—some hardcore early seventies rock and roll. I could scare them with some Zeppelin, worry them with the latest from Bowie, or maybe blow their minds with that Sly and the Family Stone record.

Instead, the first single I bought was Carole King's "So Far Away." So, it's fair to say that my pre-teen musical tastes were pretty mainstream.

As a teenager, though, I got my hands on two things that opened my mind to a universe beyond pop-rock singer-songwriters.

I got a new transistor radio almost every year. It was a radio, but you could hold it in your hand! That may not seem very exciting, but compared to most of the gifts I got for Christmas, a radio at least did *something*.

It wasn't much more high-tech than an abacus (something I *also* received one year), but it was the first thing I ever owned that gave me an escape.

When I was young, they were small models, which made them perfect for putting under my pillow while I pretended to be asleep on a school night. It wasn't so much about the music, as it was about the thrill I got listening to *anything* that was being beamed from miles away.

In Quartz Hill, California, there were only three or four local radio stations, with the most powerful of them having a mainstream commercial country music format. But if I turned the knob *very* carefully, the wonders of *amplitude modulation* brought me in touch with the whole country.

Tuning in a station with the small thumbwheel required the manual dexterity of a surgeon and the skill of an engineer, but sometimes, through the static, I could hear KOA in Denver or KSL in Salt Lake City, and on a clear night, I was able to listen to WGN in Chicago!

My first radio only had AM, then I got FM, and eventually I had a radio with *shortwave bands!* Decades before every word ever spoken was available online, this was a handheld way to learn about the world.

My first radio (and each newer, better radio) gave me my first look at places beyond the gridlines of the federally-subsidized tract homes of my Southern California youth, and it opened my ears.

I listened to Radio Havana, Radio Quito ("The Voice of the Andes!"), even Radio Moscow. Not that I spoke Spanish or Russian, but suddenly, these weren't chapters in schoolbooks. They were now real places, with real people, and real good music.

The other thing that expanded my musical horizons was my first library card. From that small county library, I began to make it my mission to check out as many albums as allowed (it might have been ten at a time), as long as they were NOT albums I knew from the radio.

So, I grabbed some jazz albums. I started with Benny Goodman, because he made me believe that it might be possible to play clarinet AND be popular. I spent a few weeks with big bands, then moved on to the smaller combos.

The first time I heard Lionel Hampton's vibraphone, with the Goodman Quartet, I was transfixed. I was amazed that an instrument, made of metal and designed to be hit with hammers, could sound so warm, and so 'cool' at the same time.

Admittedly, I didn't really know what 'cool' sounded like back then, but I knew this was 'cooler' than, say, the Carpenters. I figured I officially liked 'cool jazz,' a term I learned from the liner notes of a Modern Jazz Quartet album.

Hearing Milt Jackson's vibes work on those MJQ albums inspired me to check out more jazz albums, and eventually I decided to be adventurous and listen to some 'free jazz,' but after about a side and a half, I got scared. I wasn't ready for Ornette Coleman, and for the time being, I abandoned my nascent beatnik training.

Before I moved on from the few dozen jazz records the library had, I found an album that led me to another musical walkabout.

I was drawn in by the album cover, which, to my adolescent brain, seemed utterly subversive. Now, I realize it's just a goofy cartoon, but the piano obviously had sex with the flute, right?

French composer / pianist Claude Bolling and classical flautist Jean-Pierre Rampal created a piece called *Suite for Flute and Jazz Piano*. I wore out the grooves on the library's copy, renewing it every time it came due.

At the time, I didn't know which parts of it were supposed to be 'jazz' and which parts were 'classical,' but the combination made perfect sense to me.

Being a 'band geek,' I had some exposure to classical music, so I flipped through that section. There, I noticed an odd series of albums I checked out called *Music Minus One*. These were recordings of classical works, with one part left out, which YOU were supposed to play.

So, there was *Music Minus One Clarinet, Music Minus One Flute,* and so on. It was high-brow karaoke. I started with clarinet pieces, naturally, which led me to Mozart, which led to string quartets.

My classical education required some adjustment, since, at that time, my musical attention span was about three and a half minutes long at the time.

I was always drawn more to chamber music than the big symphonic pieces. An exception was Gershwin's "Rhapsody in Blue." It opens with a clarinet solo, for one thing.

Beyond that, although I had never been to New York, it *sounded* like New York to my teenage ears, and that was exciting. It also felt like another connection to Mom and our shared roots. It was in heavy rotation when I controlled the turntable at home.

I distinctly remember *not* enjoying Sibelius at the time. His pieces sounded gloomy to me, interrupted by occasional stretches of really loud gloom.

I get the whole melancholy thing now, but back then, it just sounded depressing. The great thing was, I could just return Sibelius to the library and try someone else.

I learned that I liked the French and Russian composers more than the Germans. I tried more modern composers like Alban Berg, but their music felt too much like schoolwork to me. I guess I was worried that if I listened to it, I might have to write a report about it.

Contemporary classical composers didn't click for me until I checked out the soundtrack to *2001: A Space Odyssey,* which led me to the music of Gyorgy Ligeti.

I didn't really understand the music any more than I understood the film, but it challenged my newly liberated ears in a way I welcomed.

Once I discovered Ligeti, I opened the door to other serious composers, all of whom were making traditional instruments do very untraditional things.

It was about this time that I stopped playing my library discoveries for my parents. I didn't think they would be into Messiaen's 'Quartet for the End of Time.'

I was a long way from Carole King, and Mom and I didn't share much, musically, until years later, when I was on my own. She called me to tell me that John Lennon had been shot.

Lennon's murder was the first celebrity death I mourned. In fact, I had just bought the *Double Fantasy* album, and was excited about the music.

It was surreal for her to have called with this news bulletin, since, to my knowledge, she wasn't a fan of the Beatles, and I'm *sure* she hadn't been following John's solo career (*"What do you think of the new Plastic Ono Band album, Mom?"*).

I understand now that Mom was trying to stay connected by sharing something that she knew was important to *me*. I was twenty, living away from home, and she knew that Lennon's death would matter to me.

Still, it seemed strange to hear *that* particular news from her. It would have made more sense if she had been calling to tell me that Andy Williams had been shot.

"If I were not a physicist,
I would probably be a musician."

--Albert Einstein

Briefcase Boy

Many years before the advent of 'nerd chic' and nerd-centric sitcoms, before the winds of nerd liberation blew across high school quads, there were just nerds. It was a time when kids didn't think it was hip to be nerdy, and nerds didn't want to be conspicuous.

This was before nerds had podcasts, or ran digital media companies, or gathered by the thousands in convention centers to celebrate their nerdiness.

Young nerds back then had to meet and communicate on the sly—casually dropping a physics book, or leaving a model U.N. badge on a cafeteria table. All the while we exchanged knowing glances that said, "Yeah, I get shoved into lockers, too."

By eighth grade, I had already established my nerd reputation—awards for 'Most Books Read,' extra credit science projects--the kinds of extracurricular activities that *invited* ridicule from my pre-pubescent peers.

If I told you I was a DJ for my junior high school's 5-watt radio station, you'd probably yell, "We have a winner! You are the least normal of all, and shall be burned in effigy by the other children!" But in retrospect, I've decided that my time spinning discs at KPRV was *incredibly* cool.

The 'on-air talent' actually had to take a test to qualify for a third class radiotelephone operator's license. The school donated some records, and one of the other kids and I brought in some 45s. I think our biggest 'hit' was Chicago's "Just You and Me." Once, we actually got into some trouble for something we played.

See, we found out that the flip side of "Goodbye Yellow Brick Road" was a song called "Young Man's Blues,' at the end of which Elton John sings 'screw you' dozens of times. We thought that was sublimely funny and played the record all the time.

Apparently, this offended the sensibilities of our broadcast region, there was a talk with some teacher, and I remember saying something precocious about 'free speech.' We stopped playing the song, but I'd like to think that it was one of the few times as a kid when I actually was a little rebellious.

That eighth-grade radio gig would be as close to hip as I would get for years. That's because, also in eighth grade, I started carrying a briefcase. I don't know why.

It couldn't have been for any practical reason, because, how much stuff did I actually have to keep organized? On the plus side, my flyers for Chess Club never got messed up.

Elmer had an old leather satchel he wasn't using. I marveled at how efficiently it held my textbooks, with everything right where I could grab it—none of that, "I can't find my math homework" nonsense for me. It even had a lock, in case . . . another eighth-grader wanted to try to steal one of my book reports.

My classmates must have marveled, too, because from then on, I was known as 'Briefcase Boy,' which is the worst superhero name *ever*. Apparently, I needed to make sure that *nobody* at school thought, even for a moment, that I was a normal boy.

If my goal was to be pushed around more, carrying a briefcase certainly made me an easier target. It's much harder to run away from a bully at the bus stop when you're trying to run with a briefcase.

Regardless of my reasons, I imagine that, in my school clothes, carrying a businessman's valise, I must have looked like a tiny Willy Loman trying to sell aluminum siding to my classmates. I was not the most popular boy in class.

Briefcase in hand, there was one thing left for me to acquire, if I wanted to ensure that I wouldn't have a social life. I needed an activity that would cement my standing within the nerd ecosystem.

No, the activity I needed to seal my fate had to be time-consuming, and ideally, it should require wearing something that would make me look unusual or silly. Fourteen-year olds are always so tolerant of that sort of thing.

Since most kids thought sports were cool, I wasn't likely to go that route. Besides, I've always been clumsy, so joining a team wasn't even on my radar. I really had only one choice open to me, if I didn't want to be a solitary nerd. I had to join something.

I chose band, which is essentially the opposite of sports. The parents signed off on the idea, so it was time to choose an instrument. Park View Junior High School didn't have an orchestra, so stringed instruments weren't an option.

The idea of playing drums was a non-starter on the home front, as were any other instruments that would be technically classified as loud—no trumpet, no trombone.

I think saxophones were in the 'too loud' category, and flutes were out, because I was getting picked on as it was—I didn't want one of my bus stop tormenters to use instrument of choice as a makeshift truncheon against me.

That left me with the clarinet. My parents watched *The Lawrence Welk Show* every Sunday night, and they had a guy who played clarinet. That was good enough for me.

The one we could afford to rent was plastic, not at all like the warm-sounding, burnished wood clarinets my classmates had, but the keys were all in the right places.

It was a Vox Ampliphonic model, which meant it had a small input where one could plug in an amplifier. That meant I could totally rock out with my clarinet, do all kinds of cool effects like you do with guitars!

Maybe I could form the first rock band with a clarinet-playing frontman! I didn't have an amplifier, and I had no understanding of what 'rocking out' meant, so none of that happened.

I got through junior high reasonably unscathed, and once I got to high school, I would be able to reinvent myself. I could tell my new friends about how I was *forced* to play clarinet, but now I think it's 'totally lame.' Anyway, I wouldn't have time for band in high school. There would be parties, I'm sure, and girls. And sports, obviously.

Or, in the first week of high school, I could sign up for both 'concert band' and *marching band*. Weirdly enough, the state of California considered marching band to be equivalent to physical education, so I got out of P.E. class all the way through high school.

But whereas concert band members could, to some extent, fly under the radar and avoid being nerd-shamed, that was *not* the case with marching band.

Looking back, the whole idea behind high school marching band sounds like a cruel sociology experiment. You take a group of kids who might be made fun of by their peers; then dress them in freakish quasi-military uniforms, often with giant furry hats, and force them to parade around in front of *the very students who make fun of them.*

We played at 'pep rallies' in the gym, and in the bleachers at football games, although I'm not sure anybody felt any 'peppier' when we were done. The reactions usually ran the gamut from oblivious to mocking, no matter how good we sounded.

During my senior year, band members were allowed to buy letter jackets, but with musical symbols on them instead of sports images.

Great—now I could be identified as a 'band geek' even when I was out of uniform. This seemed like a bad idea. I decided not to 'letter' in band.

Within the band, I got along with most of the other kids. Looking back, I think I always resented the drummers, because they seemed to have the magical ability to be in the band and still have contact with the non-band world.

They were also the 'bad boys' of high school band, but I realize that's a fairly easy bar to clear.

All snark aside, band was a formative experience for me. I'm glad I snapped on my spats, secured my chin strap, and marched. I didn't feel as alone or 'uncool' as I might have, because all I had to do was look around at rehearsal, and see rows and rows of other outcasts.

I didn't keep in touch with my band mates. This was partly because I came of age in primitive times, before the internet. Sure, *now* it's almost impossible to *avoid* hearing from an old classmate. But before we were all wired together, you had to 'write' to people to stay connected.

Typically, this 'writing' involved using a 'pen' to laboriously draw each letter by hand. Of course, you could use an early version of the smartphone called a *telephone*.

But get this—if the person you called was away from the phone, there was *no way to leave a message*! You would have to call them again and again, until they answered!

I'm not sure I would have kept in touch anyway, because, at the time, I was ready to get out of Lancaster, California faster than you can say "full-ride scholarship." When I got to UCLA, I didn't *need* to be in the band, because there were nerds everywhere!

Now, decades after I put my clarinet in its case for the last time, I find myself feeling nostalgic about band. I remembered things I hadn't flashed on in decades:

*I was chosen for All-State Honor Band. I was thirty-third chair in the clarinet section, but California **is** a big state.*

*I was asked to switch to bass clarinet, and refused because the bass clarinet parts were too boring, and after all, I **was** the thirty-third best high-school clarinetist in California.*

I played with the school Dixieland jazz group, even though I could not, in fact, improvise, which is a big part of playing jazz.

I played a marching band arrangement of the theme from 'Shaft' and realized that some music wasn't meant to be played by a marching band.

I spent hours on the practice room pianos though I could not, in fact, play piano, and was not, in fact, practicing piano but instead trying to plunk out melodies by ear and wishing I knew how to actually play piano.

I marched in 'America on Parade' for the Bicentennial at Disneyland, and felt that the 'behind the scenes' tour we got might have destroyed the magic of Disneyland for me.

As I stood at attention in the middle of a football field, attired in my bulky uniform and ridiculously tall hat, I realized that would be as close to 'sports' as I would get in high school. The moments may not have all been happy, but they were all important.

The Novelty of It

I suppose there is an intersection where nerds and pranksters overlap (hackers might be in that Venn diagram), but as a kid, I was firmly in the nerd circle, and wasn't much for doing pranks.

I *thought* of pranks and practical jokes all the time, but I wasn't wired to follow through. I was far too worried about grades, and tests, and band practice, to engage in any shenanigans. Let alone hijinks or tomfoolery.

When I was ten years old, I told the barber that I was going to be a microbiologist when I grew up. At fourteen, I had subscriptions to National Geographic *and* Scientific American.

My high school yearbook is filled with sentiments like, "I know you'll be a great doctor." My yearbook is also filled with pictures of me in various unhip groups looking ridiculously serious for a teenage boy.

It would be years before I had the slightest thought that I might be able to make other people laugh. In high school, you wouldn't have thought I had any sense of humor at all. But I was getting an education in comedy, once a week, courtesy of a DJ known as 'Dr. Demento.'

The good 'Doctor' hosted a broadcast radio show for over forty years, and on it, he played records.

These were different records than I was used to hearing. They were called 'novelty records,' and here's the deal—they were *intentionally* funny.

Novelty music wasn't accidentally funny, or funny because it was bad, or *ironically* funny—it was just meant to be funny. There were a lot of laughs, but not a lot of levels of meaning to parse with novelty songs.

I got turned on to novelty music in 1974, when Dr. D's show aired on L.A.'s KMET ("The Mighty MET"). The show went all over the comedy map. There was trippy counterculture satire from Frank Zappa, and surreal sound effects from the Spike Jones Orchestra. 'Dr. D.' introduced me to the Bransonesque humor of Ray Stevens and he introduced the world to Weird Al.

I learned every lyric to the twisted music hall pieces of Harvard mathematician Tom Lehrer ("The Masochism Tango," "Poisoning Pigeons in the Park"), and I heard vintage rock songs about purple people-eaters, and blobs, and cockroaches.

In addition, some of the songs he played stand as archival documents of trends luckily gone by. "Convoy." "Pac-Man Fever." "Valley Girl." They're like three-minute long reminders of societal groupthink gone awry.

The records he played could also be sophomoric ("Knockers Up!") or silly ("Junk Food Junkie"). And I heard records on "The Dr. Demento Show" that were downright sexual, or at least more sexual than anything I ever heard Andy Williams sing.

Where else would I have heard a song from 1946 by Jewish vaudevillian Benny Bell? "Shaving Cream" was regularly in Dr. Demento's Top Ten.

It uses what are called 'mind rhymes,' by which the listener automatically 'hears' a (usually risqué) rhyme, even though the questionable word isn't really in the lyric.

I have a sad story to tell you

It may hurt your feelings a bit

Last night when I walked into my bathroom

I stepped in a big pile of shhhhhaving cream."

When I was fourteen, that was one of the funniest things I had ever heard—*"He almost said 'shit'—that's hilarious!"*

When I was young, I also thought the following songs were funny:

"Fish Heads" by Barnes and Barnes

"Dead Skunk" by Loudon Wainwright III

"Dead Puppies" by Ogden Edsl

And for at least a year, my favorite 'song' was "They're Coming To Take Me Away, Ha Ha!" by Napoleon XIV. Of course, not everything I found funny then *stayed* funny for me.

At the time, though, *The Dr. Demento Show* gave me exactly the escape I needed from algebra, book reports, and history class. I may not have been hip to current music trends, but through novelty songs, I felt like I had the chance to be a little subversive, in my own risk-averse way.

Every Saturday night, I immersed myself in a world of weird. I memorized every record. I memorized entire Marx Brothers routines played on the show ("*Why a duck?*"). I rehearsed every Borscht Belt cadence from Allan Sherman's "Hello Muddah, Hello Fadduh," despite having never been to summer camp.

I got to know comedy records from every decade. There had already been a handful of wacky tunes that hit the charts in the pre-rock era, great songs like "Transfusion" by Nervous Norvous.

Not for nothing, the sixties also featured songs about witch doctors, and surfin' birds, and itsy-bitsy teeny-weenie yellow polka dot bikinis.

To be sure, there are acts doing funny music today, but, I believe that the golden era of goofy, musically speaking, was the nineteen seventies.

Whether it was due to post-Vietnam malaise or post-Watergate cynicism, the pop charts of that decade were littered with music ephemera, and I soaked it all in.

From the welcome-as-a-fruitcake holiday perennial, "Grandma Got Run Over By A Reindeer" to the middle-school witlessness of "My Ding-a-Ling," you couldn't tune an AM radio without hearing something silly.

Steve Martin's "King Tut" sold a million copies in 1978, and six million people bought a copy of "Disco Duck" (*a decision I'm sure at least five million of those people regret*). I'm leaving out the 1976 oddity, "Muskrat Love," because I don't think the Captain and Tennille were *trying* to be funny.

Rednecks and hillbillies even got on the seventies novelty bandwagon, with the culture clash anthem, "Uneasy Rider" and the rube romance of "Spiders and Snakes."

One of the strangest novelty songs from the seventies was by a guy named Richard 'Dickie' Goodman. "Mr. Jaws" had both of the elements needed for a topical novelty song—an easy target, and references so current they become immediately dated, locking the humor in comedy amber.

"Mr. Jaws" also might have been the first mainstream use of what is now called 'sampling.' It was such a simple formula, it's amazing nobody's really done it since.

On that record, an on-the-scene reporter is interviewing the shark from *Jaws*. That's not the weird part. The shark, called Mr. Jaws (still not the weird part), and other characters from the movie answer every question with a snippet of a pop song, to wit:

> "If someone is attacked by a shark, what should he do?"
> *"Do the hustle!"*

Not very funny out of context. Maybe it's not even that funny *in* context. My point is, it was on the radio! It was a hit! It reached #4 on Billboard's Hot 100 chart!

Novelty music is popular because it serves a purpose. Obviously, it's an escape, but any music can be an escape. Novelty music offers a very specific kind of escape.

When you escape into 'serious' music, your brain still has to do at least some work. Classical music can feel like math, and jazz requires some focus, or else it starts to sound like a bunch of people practicing different songs at the same time.

When you lose yourself in a novelty song, your brain doesn't have to do anything! It's like feeding your mind tapioca pudding.

Ultimately, a song like "My Ding-A-Ling" was a hit because it gave people four minutes and eight seconds of mental break time before having to plug in again and resume their normal, real, serious lives.

Nature, Nurture, or the Bee Gees?

I believe we are shaped by three things—our genetic makeup, the environment in which we were raised, and the pop music that was on the radio when we turned eighteen.

As a young man, I learned most of what I know about love and relationships from the songs that were popular when I graduated. I didn't date much in high school.

The musical landscape in 1978, like at any time, was a reaction to the zeitgeist. It was the year of Ted Bundy and the Hillside Strangler, and the year Son of Sam was sentenced. It was the year of Jonestown, and John Wayne Gacy, and it was the year Garfield debuted.

As a reaction to all of these horrific events, record buyers wanted something comfortable, something they understood in a world that was getting dark and crazy. Popular music in 1978 was, for the most part, soft and mushy, because the real world was hard.

Things were scary, and the last thing most Americans wanted was angry music. We wanted songs about love and dancing. I'm aware that punk music existed, and that it was important. On the other hand, the soundtrack to *Saturday Night Fever* sold fifteen million copies.

Some of the music of that decade had a profound and lasting effect on my psyche. For example, I completely avoided folk music for years after hearing Gordon Lightfoot's interminable "Wreck of the Edmund Fitzgerald."

In general, there should be a rule that folk songs have to be shorter than the events they commemorate. By the end of that song, I didn't care whether or not anyone survived.

I thought of some seventies musical nuggets recently, but the way my mind is wired, I didn't think of individual songs, where I had an ephemeral snippet of some nostalgic tune rolling around in my brain.

I get entire setlists stuck in my head, and this morning I woke up thinking of all the songs I could remember with the word 'boogie' in the title.

In case you're curious, the songs were: "Boogie Shoes," "Boogie Nights," "Boogie Fever," "Boogie Wonderland," "Boogie On Reggae Woman," "Jungle Boogie," "Get Up and Boogie," "Blame It On The Boogie," and of course, "Boogie Oogie Oogie."

Now I understand that these aren't the deepest musical sentiments ever expressed, and it's been a few years since I put on my *my my my my my boogie shoes,*' but I think these seemingly lightweight records actually point to something heavy.

All of the above boogie-centric songs charted between 1974 and 1979. Though my late teen years had their share of global issues and incidents, I don't remember ever worrying about a worldwide economic collapse or crypto-Islamic terrorists. You wanna know what I remember from the news in the seventies? Lines at gas stations were long.

My point is, there have always been scary things in the world, but now half the planet is trafficking in fear, like fear should have its own NASDAQ symbol. I believe this is because nobody is writing songs about the *boogie* anymore, or boogieing, or other boogie related behavior.

On a side note, whatever happened to the 'woogie?' In the forties, people were known to 'boogie-woogie.' When World War II ended, did people just abandon their woogie? Could that be why America is in decline?

Some historians now believe that the Allies won the war in part because they could both boogie and woogie. They truly were the 'greatest generation.'

Getting back to the seventies, when disco was a part of the musical landscape, the world was a safer place. We weren't involved in multiple wars when we were digging Donna Summer. Coincidence?

In addition, I'll go so far as to say that disco was a great cultural equalizer, because almost everyone looked stupid dancing to it.

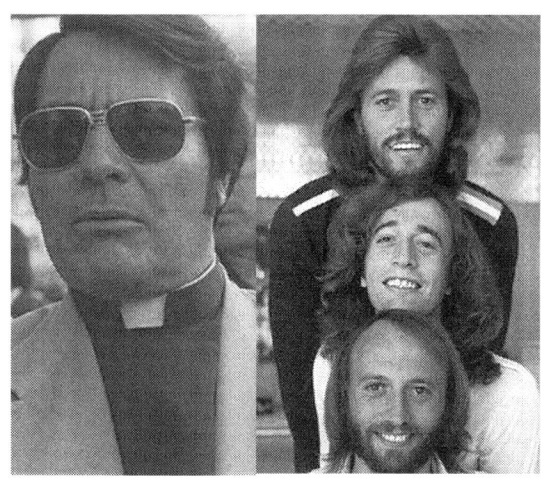

Which picture is more frightening?

When I turned eighteen, six of the top ten songs on the charts were either performed, written or produced by some combination of Bee Gees. Whether it was Barry, Maurice, Robin, or Andy, over half of the top ten songs in the country were sung in a quivering falsetto.

To this day, I can't walk down a street in Brooklyn carrying a paint can without hearing the harmonies of the Brothers Gibb and the incessant, mind-numbing rhythm of 103 beats per minute. It's a good thing I don't paint, or live in Brooklyn.

I think my lack of early romantic success was directly related to the songs that were filling my head at the time. Without siblings to ask for advice, I had to rely on the radio to understand dating, and I took the lyrics of every song to heart. Except Steely Dan songs. I *still* have no idea what those lyrics meant.

Mid-seventies pop music taught me life lessons. I figured out early that, if you weren't cool enough to be *fooling around* with girls yet, you could at least *hold* one--during a slow dance.

The best scenario would be to already be on the dance floor when the DJ switches from a fast song to a slow one. Then, you didn't have to *ask* for a slow dance--she's already there, and if you can summon the confidence just to put your hands on her hips, she might let you move in a circle like that for a few minutes while she looks everywhere but at you.

If you're really lucky, and they play the 'live' version of Earth, Wind & Fire's "Reasons," she's stuck with you for *eight minutes and thirty-two seconds*. That's almost as long as a date.

I learned some fundamental truths from pop music. From my radio, I learned that "Love Is Thicker Than Water," except when "Love Is Like Oxygen." I learned that some women are actually "Three Times A Lady," which scared me.

Without pop music, I would have never *heard* of the "Serpentine Fire," which, looking back on it, probably caused the tragic "Disco Inferno."

And though, at the time, I may not have understood what "Night Fever" was, I was pretty sure you could catch it from "Shadow Dancing."

I learned to ask questions in relationships, like "How Deep Is Your Love?" I realized that "You Can't Turn Me Off (In The Middle Of Turning Me On)."

I prepared myself for a lifetime of settling when I heard that "Two Out Of Three Ain't Bad." I also learned that it's entirely possible to be "Bluer Than Blue."

Only later did I realize that the songs of my youth weren't always applicable to my life. Despite what Mick Jagger says in "Miss You," when I've gone through a breakup, I've never had a friend call to say, 'We're gonna come around at twelve with some Puerto Rican girls that's just *dying* to meet you'."

Not every lesson the radio taught me resonated for me. Sadly, I've never had the chance to visit "Thunder Island," and to this day, I'm hazy about where, exactly, "The Groove Line" is. But if the songs from my youth taught me anything, it's that "Grease" is the word.

*"Musicals had a good, happy feeling.
It's not reality, but who cares?
There's too much reality these days."*

--Shirley Jones

Upstaging Myself

You know that person who sings along with *every* song that comes on the radio? The one who not only sings along with the singing part but with the guitar solos too, and then tells you trivia about the song, and then wants you to listen to a mix CD he made of music that has the same 'vibe'?

I'm that guy. I know, it's bad enough that I actually use the word 'vibe'. But worse, to some people, is the fact that I am constantly singing something. So far, most of my friends have been enthusiastically tolerant.

I don't need an audience or a microphone to sing. I sing when I'm cooking, I sing when I take out the trash, I sing in the bathtub.

I've been known to sing along, full-voiced, with a particularly catchy carpet commercial *('Eight hundred, five-eight-eight, two-three hundred . . .').*

I sometimes think I get more from singing along than I do from singing. It's the *'along'* part, the shared experience, that can really make the music heal you. In the bigger picture, in our polarized world, joining the chorus could do us all some good.

That's because, as long as the music keeps playing, if you're singing with other people, you don't care about their politics, or their religion. By definition, if you're singing the same song, you need to be on the same page.

One night, I had the chance to sing at the Hollywood Bowl. This wasn't onstage, mind you, because that wasn't the point of the evening. Onstage, a giant screen showed the Oscar-winning film *The Sound of Music,* while over ten thousand people in the audience *sang along with the entire movie.*

It was truly weird to hear *that* many people attempting to yodel in unison during "Lonely Goatherd," and it was silliness on a grand scale when we all waved sprigs of edelweiss. Essentially, it all turned *Sound of Music* into a safer version of *Rocky Horror.*

During all of this, thousands of people were acting with one intent, and they were creating their own happiness. Sure, the lyrics on the screen made it easier, but most of us knew those already.

I first discovered the joys of 'singing along' in my mid-twenties, when I walked into a non-descript hotel bar. I had just moved to Minneapolis, and since I didn't know anybody, my evenings were relatively free.

I walked into this bar, mostly because I needed someplace to sit and figure out why I had just moved to Minneapolis.

It was decorated in mid-century musty, with a piano in the middle of the bar, and stools around the piano. There were only a few people drinking, and most of those were sitting on the stools, flipping through binders.

From what I could tell, these books contained the songs the piano player knew how to play—and here's the beauty part: apparently, anyone could just drunkenly shout one of the titles from the book, and this lady would play it! And everybody sang along!

I had never gotten through to the request line of any radio station, but here was the live equivalent. Fortunately, I knew some songs that were popular before I was born, because the songbook reflected the bar's demographic, and I was youngest person in the room by at least twenty years.

In addition to the singalong standards like "It's A Sin To Tell A Lie," every so often someone would be handed a microphone for a solo. Obviously, I like attention. So, once I got the feel of the place, I dove in.

I had learned the song "Be My Love," made famous by the operatic tenor turned popular singer, Mario Lanza (think a fifties-era Josh Groban). Now I wasn't Lanza, but, before I smoked cigarettes, I could hit the occasional high note to some effect.

Twenty-four year old me would walk up the piano player, whisper "'Be My Love--in the original key," and electrify a room full of sixty-year-olds drinking Manhattans. Okay, so 'electrify' is probably too strong, but the old people definitely dug me.

Piano bars are a lost part of our cultural landscape, and I think it's a shame. I'm a huge fan of the idea of a group of random strangers getting together to sing the same song, in unison (with a little bit of drunk harmonizing on a really good night).

Nobody argues, nobody judges, no politics . . . all that matters is the "Sentimental Journey."

To many people, piano bars are just one tiny step above karaoke bars in the entertainment hierarchy. In fairness, though, I've never had a problem with karaoke. Obviously, it's a chance to sing, but I'll take it a step further and say that karaoke provides a public service.

It allows someone who isn't a professional entertainer to experience the tribal pat on the back called applause. As a performer, I've been lucky enough to occasionally hear applause for things I've done. People who didn't know me, getting together as a group to tell me, "Good job!"

The working-class guy singing Journey at the VFW *only* gets to experience that rush on karaoke night. I understand, it can be challenging to endure the parade of Gaga wannabes, and nobody needs to hear six frat boys drunkenly bellowing the wrong lyrics for "Born to Be Wild."

On the other hand, sometimes you get to see some CPA cut loose and channel his inner Elvis for three minutes, and it makes me feel good to see someone get a response he will never get at his job, no matter *how* good he is as an accountant.

I think it's great that people who don't normally get praise from strangers can do karaoke and, if everyone is drunk enough, get a crowd cheering for them. Sometimes, everybody can use a bit of audible validation.

Whether it's drunk amateurs at karaoke, melancholy middle-agers in piano bars, or just me, Fleetwood Mac and the vacuum cleaner, I've never had a problem with the concept of 'breaking into song for no apparent reason.' I suppose that's why I've always loved musical theater.

I have friends who loathe musicals, and their argument is always the same: musicals aren't realistic. Apparently, most people don't spontaneously sing their thoughts and feelings in real life! To which I say, "Maybe they should."

Would it be so bad if the clerk at the grocery store gave you a musical number while ringing up your purchase? Maybe a heartfelt ode to working for minimum wage?

Some restaurants have singing waiters—why not singing auto mechanics? *"Your repairs should take about twenty minutes, so here's a medley from West Side Story."*

I can imagine a whole new approach to therapy. It might be off-putting at first, but singing about your issues could help you break through those repressed feelings from childhood. Every shrink's office could have a small upright piano.

As to the complaint that musicals aren't realistic, I'd like to suggest that realism isn't *really* a necessary part of entertainment.

If you watch a play, you hear long monologues delivered by actors, when in 'real life,' somebody would probably interrupt them, or tell them to shut up.

You can make a film *look* as 'realistic' as you want, but people aren't really as clever as screenwriters make them. Also, movies have spaceships and time machines. Not to put too fine a point on it, but I think there's enough real life in real life.

I spend enough time watching news from the real world, so I don't need my entertainment to always be 'realistic.' I need regular breaks from reality, because frankly, reality can be tedious as hell.

The first time I performed onstage without a clarinet in my hands was the summer before senior year. It had nothing to do with a desire to be onstage, and everything to do with my mom wanting me out of the house for the summer.

I was an academic overachiever and, for the first time, there were no summer school classes that I hadn't already taken. I was facing a summer with nothing to do except read the encyclopedia, or work on that new language I was planning to invent. I had to find something to occupy myself until September.

As it happened, every summer, the local junior college produced a musical, and anyone in the community could audition. That summer, it was *The Music Man,* which tells a tale of marching bands and romance set in small-town Iowa.

It's arguably the least edgy musical in the entire American musical theater canon. A musical about the history of Jell-O would have more 'grit.' The Beatles recorded the show's impossibly sappy love song, "Till There Was You."

I didn't care about any of that. I was simply trying to fill my summer. Also, though Mom and I were close, we both had strong personalities, and a little separation was becoming a good idea. I decided to audition, and she was fine with that.

I was cast in the chorus, which in itself was amazing, since I had, at that point, never acted, or sung in public, and I couldn't dance.

Then, through a fluke (somebody who had been cast dropped out in the first week of rehearsal), I was asked to be in the barbershop quartet of the show, which involved singing in almost every number.

Of course, there was dancing. Lots of shopkeepers and townsfolk doing high kicks and twirls. The exception to all this joyous choreography was the barbershop quartet, who stood by the mayor's podium.

Entirely because of my spectacular mediocrity at dancing, the director decided the barbershop quartet would be better off just standing there. I didn't mind—I was singing.

It would be a few years before I would toss away *all* of my academic potential, but the experience I had in the Antelope Valley Junior College production of *The Music Man* lit the fuse. That's because in theater, I found a place that was even *more* welcoming of misfits than high school band.

This changed my life. I don't mean that I bought a straw hat and joined the Society for the Preservation and Encouragement of Barbershop Quartet Singing in America. .

What I mean is that, at the time, I thought of performing as just another extracurricular activity, like Debate Club or the school newspaper.

The entertainment business wasn't my calling, I told myself, because it's too hard to make a *living* at it. Which, as it turns out, may be accurate, but that's beside the point. Anyway, with my grades and test scores, I just assumed I was supposed to become a doctor. *Spoiler alert: I did not become a doctor.*

I did a couple of shows during my senior year of high school, but when I got to UCLA, I still viewed theater as, at best, a hobby, and at worst, a distraction.

I was there to learn organic chemistry, and advanced calculus, and whatever else it was you learned before you learned how to be a doctor.

My favorite role as a young actor was when I had a chance to understudy the lead role in Gilbert and Sullivan's *The Pirates of Penzance*. With apologies to Shakespeare, in this case, the play *wasn't* the thing. The *thing* was, for this part, I learned how to fight with a sword!

That was exponentially cooler than anything I ever learned in biology class! I only played 'Frederick' in one performance, and it was for an audience of middle-school kids, but, come on— I got to sing AND fight with a sword!

Since college, I've only been in one theatrical show. It was another musical, called *The 1940s Radio Hour,* and appropriately, I played a comic who really wants to be a singer. I wasn't much of an actor, but *that* role was definitely within my range.

The show as written is a big-hearted piece of fluff, and I didn't have to dance, so I was thrilled to do it.

We did a 'bus and truck' tour, covering several states (I think we did the show in *both* Dakotas), with venues ranging from old folks' groups to the twenty-four hundred seat Kentucky Center for the Arts.

On some level, all performers are children, and I learned during our several weeks of touring that I don't always play well with other children. The cast was filled with talented people, but two months of bus travel with the same egos on board was a challenge.

By the end of the tour, I spent most of my bus time playing dominoes with the old guy who played 'Pops,' drinking airline-sized bottles of whisky. But on stage, I was singing every night.

The coolest part of that was the show's 'big band.' *The 1940's Radio Hour* used vintage arrangements for the songs, and period microphones, so for my one solo number ('Blue Moon'), when I stood in front of our horn section at the bandstand, it felt like I was travelling through time.

Since I was playing a comic relief role in the show, the high point in my big song involved a sight gag. For this gag, my pants fell down as I sang the end of 'Blue Moon' in my boxers.

Sure people were laughing, but as far as I was concerned, I was a professional singer, and people were applauding my vocalizing, not my underwear.

Then a comic friend told me about a bar in Minneapolis called the Gay 90s. She said they had an open mic every Thursday, This wasn't karaoke, but a place where an actual piano player accompanied you. And you could do songs from musicals!

She let me know that "The Gay 90s" was, in fact, a gay bar, which I had already surmised, and which wasn't an issue for me.

Turns out, when you do theater, you run into the occasional gay person, so the environment didn't faze me. Besides, I was bisexual, although I'm not sure I knew it at the time.

For a little clarification, the 90s is not just a 'gay bar.' A better word would be 'emporium.' There was a lot going on there—downstairs bar, dance floor, drag show room, leather room, and most importantly, a piano bar.

Jazz vocalist Lori Dokken held court once a week for their open mic, and somehow brought together a motley group of people representing the full spectrum of sexuality and varying degrees of mental 'health.'

On a more superficial level, if one of the less experienced singers on the sign-up sheet proved to be . . . pitch-challenged, Lori would do a couple numbers to cleanse everyone's musical palate.

The day I leaned of my mom's passing, I needed to sing. Lori was playing a hotel gig downtown, and I wandered into the lounge. I asked if she'd play Billy Joel's "New York State of Mind" in Gloria's honor, and Lori invited me up to sing.

As I was shell-shocked (and not a professional singer), it's probably just as well that there wasn't an audience. Honestly, my recollection is that it was more therapy than performance,

Either way, I was grateful for the session .It was especially gratifying to know that I could get more 'therapy' with Lori at the 90s whenever I needed it.

When I first went to the 90s, I was oblivious to my own orientation, I'm sure there were signs along the way that I somehow missed.

For instance, now that I think of it, I remember being a good deal more into Shaun Cassidy than my friends. Now that I think of it, I don't remember dating a lot of girls.

But I had recently started my standup career, and during the standup boom of the mid-eighties, a guy telling a joke on a stage could actually get laid. By women. Not as often as musicians got laid, but often enough to convince me I played for Team Hetero.

So when I went to the Gay 90s, I figured I was a just a straight guy who really appreciated the music of Stephen Sondheim. Eventually, I put the pieces together and realized that my vague bisexual inklings weren't that vague and were more than inklings. Who knew?

The reality is, my visits to The 90s probably helped me get comfortable with my sexuality, but a much more significant development happened there. I came out of the closet as a singer.

After that, I found myself being pulled into that world. I started to seek out places where singers gathered, and, shockingly, I began to prefer the company of singers. There were places called 'cabarets' where, once you knew your way around, you could sing *two* songs back to back!

The Oasis in North Hollywood, Marie's Crisis in Greenwich Village, Davenport's in Chicago . . . whenever I moved, the first place I sought was wherever the singers went. I would let the piano player know I wanted to sing, and wait for my turn at the mic.

Some musicians who host open mic nights for singers appreciate that I can do standup, because they can take a longer break if I do a little comedy.

In return for essentially stalling between singers, and playing to a room full of other singers who were mostly looking at their music, they might let me do *three* songs.

At least at the beginning, three songs was pushing it, since the only song I knew well enough to do in public was "Summertime" from Gershwin's *Porgy and Bess*. It's a touching ballad and a heart-rending lullaby, although not necessarily when I sang it.

Eventually, I learned a few more songs, because audiences (especially ones comprised of other singers) don't always want to hear "Summertime."

Then I noticed singers were bringing in sheet music and putting their music in binders, and I thought, I need more music. And sheet protectors. And a binder.

Everything came full circle one day when I was in the Chicago Public Library, checking out collections like *Show Tunes for the Male Voice* and *Greatest Broadway Showstoppers*.

Suddenly a part of me was back at the county library in Lancaster, checking out vinyl albums and filling my head with music.

Just like with marching band, I had found my people. These were people who talked of 'writing out charts' and 'going to the bridge,' and who knew you had to have an up-tempo to go with a slow song.

With my 'book' in hand, I *felt* like a singer. I knew I wasn't as technically proficient as other singers, but once in a while I could *sell* a song, even if I couldn't *sing* it.

The best thing about a cabaret is that, when you're singing, the audience is right there, close enough to touch.

I'm a bit less active than I used to be, with my various old man infirmities, so my book and I don't get out much these days. I've *watched* a few musicals on stage, and when I have, it took all the self-restraint I had to *not* sing along.

I haven't been to a karaoke bar in years, which is also probably related to my age. I don't quite have the patience I used to have, so waiting through seventeen singers so that I can do Roy Orbison's "Crying" isn't as appealing.

I would still go to piano bars, but they're becoming as hard to find as video stores. I suppose millennials have trouble with the concept of just sitting around a piano and singing along, without ironic detachment and snark.

I may not be singing in public much, but I still sing. To myself, mostly, although I'm sure the neighbors have had a chance to enjoy my version of Springsteen's "Thunder Road."

For their benefit, I try to keep the show tunes to a minimum, unless *The Sound of Music* is on TV. At which point, everyone will just have to accept that I will be singing along on every number except "The Lonely Goatherd."

Traveling Music

It's always seemed weird to me, this idea of choosing a song to represent an entire state. Off the top of your head, can you name your state's official song? If you're in Tennessee, I'll cut you some slack, since *seven* songs have official status there.

In contrast, New Jersey has, thus far, opted out, having never designated an official State Song. It would be a hard song to write, since a New Jersey state song would need to set organized crime to music, and find something that rhymes with political corruption.

Of the forty-nine official state songs, an astonishing *two* were written by John Denver. Every so often I have to remind myself how freakishly popular John Denver was.

Seven states were lazy, and chose songs which could be called "Insert State Name Here." There's not much of a distinction between "Alabama," "Illinois," "Montana," and the other songs in this group.

They mostly sound like graduation marches, and the lyrics usually make some reference to mountains, unless the state doesn't have mountains, in which case, lakes are probably mentioned.

Oklahoma put in zero effort, adopting the song "Oklahoma" from the musical 'Oklahoma.'

> *"Governor, we need to commission someone to write a song for the state--a song that captures the essence of the land and its people."*
>
> *"Yeah, didn't someone write a song about us already? The one from that play--just use that one."*

The best state song *title,* in my mind, is New Mexico's "Land of Enchantment," which is also the state motto, which is a whole other thing states adopt. I like "Land of Enchantment" because it sounds like the name of a Moody Blues album.

The title of the California state song is "I Love You, California," which sounds appropriately huggy-kissy for the state, but also a little too casual for my tastes. It might as well be called "I Love You, *Babe*."

Although I'm a native Californian, I am reasonably certain that I have neither sung nor heard "I Love You, California," but I found the lyrics. It starts off covering a lot of ground . . .

I love you, California, you're the greatest state of all.
I love you in the winter, summer, spring and in the fall.
I love your fertile valleys; your dear mountains I adore.
I love your grand old ocean and I love her rugged shore.

You've got your ocean, your valleys, and naturally, your mountains. By the fourth verse, though, the writer starts running out of big ideas. with the line, "I love you, Tamalpais." Also known as 'Mt. Tam,' 'Tamalpais is only a bit over twenty-five hundred feet in elevation, so it's really more of a hill.

I spent the first twenty-four years of my life in California, and while "I Love You ,California" would make a decent postcard, no single song could possibly describe the state. I really only know Southern California, but even with just half the state to cover, one song isn't enough.

A Los Angeles playlist, for me, would be all about the city's bipolarity. Every time I went back, it would be cuddly Disney tunes mashed up with the synth hooks of Wall of Voodoo.

To me, L.A. always sounded like an unexpected jam session featuring The Doors and the Carpenters. It's the Beach Boys' achingly wistful "Warmth of the Sun" mashed up with the dystopia of David and David's "Welcome to The Boomtown."

There were days in Los Angeles that sounded like the Go-Gos, and nights that sounded like the Red Hot Chili Peppers, at least their early stuff. If I wandered too far from my comfort zone, L.A. started to sound like N.W.A.

When I wrote this, I lived in Portland, Oregon. By the time you read it, I might be living in Des Moines, Iowa. I truly have no idea. Chances are, I'm either packing or unpacking something right now.

If you think of my life in terms related to Bob Dylan (and I do), then I'm on my Never Ending Tour. Like Bob's, my 'tour' began in the eighties, had moments that were ragged and uneven in the nineties, and was marked by erratic indifference in the 2000s.

Also like Dylan, I've tried to reinvent myself numerous times, and like Bob, I haven't always been successful. In my defense, none of *my* attempts at a fresh start were as poorly received as Dylan's 'gospel' period.

Whenever I decided I needed rebranding, I would choose a city, do some reading, and then try to figure out if I knew anyone there, or *knew* anyone who knew anyone. I would also start diving into the music of wherever I was going.

When I got there, I would already have headphones on, listening to a playlist of songs about that city, or by artists from there.

Somehow, at the turn of the millennium, I ended up in Boston. The year I was there, I was as close to insane as one could be while still performing and having something of a social life. I was a click or two away from an official diagnosis, a tiny cup of meds, and paper slippers.

Other than that Aerosmith gig I may or may not have seen, I have very few musical memories of Boston. There was no room in my head to retain any music, what with all the crazy in there at the time. I realize now that if I had sought out some music, I might have been able to better manage my crazy.

I do have one faint, barely audible musical memory of my year in Boston. I saw the Boston Pops give a holiday concert in a historic old church. I hang onto this memory because it has enough good elements to balance my otherwise regrettable time there.

First, it was Christmas music, which has always made me happy, even after I converted to Judaism. It was the also the Boston *Pops*, which meant I heard wonderful orchestral sounds, but didn't have to work as hard as I would have with a more 'serious' orchestra. They didn't play anything *too* challenging or adventurous. I didn't need to hear anything *too* challenging.

I tried moving to New York three times, and each time New York slapped me down. I don't blame New York. My most recent Manhattan misadventure was almost certainly my fault.

For some reason, when I ran the numbers, I decided four hundred dollars would be enough to get me set up in the most expensive city in the country. With no job. That's when I realized I would not make a very good life coach.

Only two memories of New York resonate for me musically, and they couldn't feel more different to me. The first time, in my twenties, it's a memory of *Sweeney Todd* at Circle in the Square Theater.

I was in theater geek heaven. First, it was theater "in the round,' and the actors came into the audience, so it was intimate and visceral. During the "City on Fire" number, you really felt there were "lunatics yelling in the streets." Of course, we were in New York, so it's possible they weren't actors at all, just lunatics.

The music was intimate, too, with no orchestra. Instead, there were three synthesizers playing the entire score, which allowed me to focus on trying to follow Sondheim's complicated and fast-moving and overlapping lyrics.

This was definitely Advanced Musical Theater 101. Oh, and there was Angela Lansbury, who would be worth it if she were on roller-skates singing songs from *Xanadu*.

The antithesis of that musical high happened toward the end of my last 'visit.' When my four hundred dollars turned out to be somewhat less than I needed to make a go of it, I resorted to a time-honored method of getting on my feet. I sold my CDs.

In the digital music era, I'm not sure what people do when they run out of money, but in my day, you could always make a few bucks by selling your albums to a used music store.

You would bring them to the counter, where some kid would ruthlessly assign a value to each disc, checking for scratches, and judging your musical taste.

All the music I had carefully chosen to raise my spirits and inspire me on my journey was now being appraised by someone who wasn't old enough to have heard of it.

The worst part of the process was discovering how little *my* music was worth to someone else. Two bucks for Laura Nyro and Labelle's classic *Gonna Take A Miracle?* Are you kidding me?

Still, I needed the two dollars, and the other twenty dollars I garnered from the rest of my collection. One of the last memories I have of New York is of looking longingly at the store through the window of the M50 bus. I just hope whoever bought that Nyro album understands how great it is.

I've lived in Chicago twice. During the first night of my first time there, I did what I usually do when I'm new in town—I found the nearest piano bar. I grabbed a seat near the tip jar at a place called Davenport's.

Intimate and rambunctious in equal measure, it's the kind of joint where the wait staff sings, the bartender sings (and sometimes plays violin while standing on the bar), and on open mic night, you might hear everything from an Italian aria to a Garth Brooks tune.

It will always be my 'home club,' no matter where I technically reside, because it embodies the best qualities of music. It somehow manages to include phenomenal talent, without ever feeling intimidating to the dabblers among us. The phrase *'nurturing bar'* might seem like an oxymoron, but that's the vibe.

It's a bar remarkably devoid of annoying drunks, though many nights, I was both drunk and annoying. Even then, they treated me like family—if your family has any annoying drunks, you understand.

Open mic Mondays were a fabulous gallimaufry, with George Howe as ringleader at the piano. George's job on Mondays is to accompany all of the singers who have signed up to sing. No matter how *well* they sing.

In addition, he has to figure out a key for the song if the singers don't have music with them. Then there's the most daunting aspect of the gig. He has to deal with the egos of all the singers.

I imagine it's like herding second-graders, except that you can give a second-grader a time out. Also, second-graders rarely insist on belting "Summertime."

When I came back to Chicago in 2006, I was a better singer, but the rest of my life was distinctly out of tune. In my forties at that point, I was something of a lost soul.

The standup scene had changed, and I wasn't a part of it. I also didn't have a lot of marketable skills beyond joke-telling, which is only marketable when you're actually *working* as a comedian.

I was constantly broke, and damn near broken. I also see now that being around me then wasn't easy. When every third sentence starts with "Can you help me," people stop wanting to hang with you, and I get that now.

As toxic as I was then, Davenport's, and George, still welcomed me for my two songs every Monday night. At that point, I'm sure my performances seemed more like therapy than art.

In retrospect, everyone might have been better off if I had spent my Monday nights *in* therapy. Undoubtedly, I would have lost the remaining pieces of my mind if I hadn't had a place where I could sing through my crazy on a weekly basis.

As tired as I am of moving *anywhere*, I intend to get back to Chicago. It'll be a stop on *my* Never Ending Tour. I just need to find the right songs to sing, an up-tempo and a ballad, preferably with lyrics about paying off debts and making amends.

Minnesota Revisited

The first time I moved to Minnesota, it was 1984, and a plucky, upstart tech company named Apple released something called a Macintosh. Ronald Reagan was re-elected, winning every state in the union *except* Minnesota. I voted for Mondale, so I'd like to think I helped him win his ten electoral votes.

In music news, Prince had two Top 100 singles, "When Doves Cry" and "Let's Go Crazy." Since both of those became hits right after I moved to his home state, I'd like to believe I helped with that, too.

Minnesota has always been the place I go when I don't know where *else* to go. Maybe it's the air up there, or the lakes, or maybe I simply have a fondness for emotionally repressed Scandinavians. I *am* Danish, so maybe it's in my genetic code.

Whatever the reasons, I've moved there three times. I see the places I've lived as dating partners, and Minneapolis is that first love after moving away from home. Even though a long-term relationship wasn't in the cards for us, she's always been there to comfort me when a sexier city broke my heart.

I find it helpful to describe the places I've lived in terms of the mental illness that place represents. In that respect, if L.A. is bipolar, then the entire state of Minnesota has dissociative identity personality disorder.

Minnesota is responsible for the 'Minneapolis sound,' which was a template for eighties and nineties r&b, but it was also the home of Judy Garland. The Andrews Sisters started harmonizing in Minnesota, and The Replacements started drinking there.

Minnesota embraces the gentle self-parody of *A Prairie Home Companion and* supports the innovative hip hop labels Doomtree and Rhymesayers. You have to appreciate any place where Garrison Keillor and Brother Ali are neighbors.

The Suburbs are described in Wikipedia as a "punk rock/funk/new wave" band, which is as good a label as any, if you need to label your music. Speaking of labels, The Gear Daddies and the Jayhawks were 'alt-country' thirty years before the Avett Brothers.

No place in Minnesota has ever been called "Funkytown," but in 1980, we went there musically, thanks to a Minnesotan with the distinctly *unfunky* name of Steven Greenberg, a former Miss Black Minnesota named Cynthia Johnson, and a band called 'Lipps, Inc.'

If you can't picture hardcore punk thriving in the land of 'Minnesota nice,' listen to three minutes of early Hüsker Dü. For that matter, "Surfin' Bird" by the Trashmen had punk DNA (it was covered by The Ramones). Both Hüsker Dü and The Trashmen recorded at Soma Records in Minneapolis, twenty years apart.

None of this explains Bob Dylan. I've learned that following Dylan is a lot like driving through Minnesota—once you get past how cold and forbidding the terrain is, if you dig deeply enough, you find at least ten thousand reasons to keep exploring.

Bob Dylan was only a Minnesotan for the first nineteen years of his life, growing up in Hibbing, then spending a couple of years in the Dinkytown folk scene around the campus of the University of Minnesota. Still, if I can call myself at least part-Minnesotan, Dylan definitely qualifies.

Somehow, through musical alchemy, he took his formative Minnesota years, channeled a mystical bond with Woody Guthrie, took a trip to New York, and emerged as the brilliant, sloppy, visionary, aloof, adventurous, lazy, important, and confounding artist known as Bob Dylan.

I'm no Dylanologist, and there is nothing I can write about Dylan that hasn't already been written by scholars and contradicted by The Bob himself. I don't claim to understand why he pursued various creative paths that, more often than not, left either critics or fans shaking their heads.

Thirty-six studio albums, and for at least half of them, Bob sounds like he just rolled out of bed with some random stream of consciousness that he scrawled on a bar napkin the night before.

Normally, I don't care much for artists who don't care much for their audience. With Dylan, though, his disdain always felt like tough love, and I think that's how he means it.

Only Dylan has the capacity to seem artistically vital while in the same moment seeming colossally bored. He's that rare artist who is interesting precisely because he doesn't care whether you think he's interesting.

He *could* have mixed in a few of his hits when he did his gospel tours, to make the whole born-again thing more accessible to us heathens, but he wanted to challenge us.

He *could* play "Tangled Up In Blue" in concert the way it sounds on the record, but he knows that that would be too easy, and we wouldn't learn anything it from it.

Sure, Dylan could have chosen *not* to record a Christmas album, but he felt like making a Christmas album, whether *we* wanted one or not. Now, I don't feel that holiday warmth until I hear Bob plow through "Must Be Santa," like he's on a manic, drunken toboggan ride.

When he was David Letterman's final musical guest, he *could* have given a dignified reading of one of his iconic works, like "Blowin' In The Wind." Instead, he croaked his way through a Sinatra tune. It was a great choice, but Bob didn't care whether we thought so.

My favorite story from Bob's career involves the recording of 'Blonde on Blonde.' Dylan insisted on jacking up the treble on the sound board, creating an unusually bright and edgy sound.

The engineer lobbied for more of a balance between bass and treble, but Bob explained that his way, the music would sound better coming out of car speakers, and that was where people listen to the radio.

Every few years, some new artist with a guitar and a thesaurus is called 'the next Dylan' by the rock press. I haven't spent much time checking out 'Dylanesque' singer-songwriters, because the real deal is still making music.

To me, the most amazing thing about Dylan's career is that, no matter *what* he does musically, he remains a part of the conversation. There is still a buzz about any new Bob Dylan album release, even if that new album is a collection of outtakes from sessions recorded in the analog era.

At seventy-four, he released the moody, stripped-down *Shadows in the Night*, and *that* album hit #7 on the Billboard chart. But he hasn't become just an act on the 'oldies' circuit, spoon-feeding his hits to adoring crowds.

He still rearranges and reconstructs old 'favorites' when he plays live, inspiring fans in attendance to mutter, things like *"I think he's playing 'Chimes of Freedom,' but I can't quite tell."* He still has the power to aggravate audiences, and a sure test of an artist's vitality is the ability to provoke a reaction.

Dylan's lyrical output has been as diverse as his musical journeys, but I've always been especially fond of his dreamscapes. "Motorpsycho Nitemare." "Talkin' World War III Blues." Early in his career, he recorded "Bob Dylan's Dream" *and* "Bob Dylan's 115th Dream," and sometimes, when I need a surrealism fix, I go back to these tracks.

Hopefully, on some future "Bootleg Series" release, we'll learn about the hundred and thirteen dreams that came in between.

I've never numbered my dreams (surprising, with my OCD), but I'm sure at least one of them was inspired by Dylan. Probably that one where I'm driving a Cadillac past a fallout shelter with Abraham Lincoln.

I hope that as long as Bob Dylan dreams, he'll continue to write down those dreams, and occasionally strap on his harmonica and guitar to share them.

It's always hard to imagine Dylan having much more to say, but then, every few years, he releases an album with a handful of songs that say something new, or say something old in a new way.

Who knows? Maybe when Bob is ninety, we'll see *The Bootleg Series Vol 28*. He also might decide to annoy everybody, by being a guest mentor on The Voice, or authorizing a Broadway musical about his early years called *Blowin'!*

Maybe he'll have converted to Islam. I can imagine a ninety-something Dylan saying, "God wears different suits, depending on where he has to go that day," or something similarly cryptic.

He could conceivably reappear with a collection of duets with Prince. The album could be called *U Belong 2 Minnesota*, and I would buy it, or download it, or have it surgically implanted in my ear—however we're consuming music by then.

There is also a distinct possibility that Bob Dylan will simply become a cranky old man. He's been one before. He was always ambivalent about being the 'voice of a generation,' so he might just get persnickety and release an album called, *The World Is Screwed, So Leave Me Alone.*

I have a recurring dream in which I'm seeing Dylan in concert for the first time. He's doing all of my favorites (of course none of them sound the original recordings), when it becomes apparent that he can't find his harmonica.

In the dream, I happen to have a harmonica, so I give it to him. Then, a hologram of Woody Guthrie joins him onstage, and things get weird.

"Music is the only religion that delivers the goods."

--Frank Zappa

Ticket Stubs

I don't have many souvenirs. Some of that can be attributed to how often I've moved. Sometimes I was moving toward something, like a good comedy scene, or a really hot woman I met after a show. Sometimes I was moving away from something, like creditors, or winter. Either way, I had to travel lightly.

So, I probably have bits and pieces of personal ephemera scattered around the country that I haven't bothered to reacquire. What I *don't* have are any mementos of the concerts I've seen. I've never felt the need to hang on to ticket stubs.

It's not as if, when I tell people I saw the Ramones in 1978, they're going to insist on proof that I was there. As for myself, I don't need a tangible reminder that I was at a show, because if it was memorable . . . I would remember it.

It helps that I haven't been to a huge number of concerts. As much as I love music, in fifty-plus years, I haven't been to many live shows. That's because I rarely have that extra twenty, or fifty, or hundred dollars when someone I wanted to hear came to town.

I've probably *opened* for more rock bands than I've seen as an audience member. Opening for a rock band is usually grim work for a comedian, because most people don't want to hear someone talk for twenty minutes before they get to hear the *music* they actually *paid* to hear. As a comic, the best case scenario is that the crowd is quietly annoyed.

I had the opportunity to open for the eighties band, The Romantics. The Romantics had approximately two hits, "That's What I Like About You" and the one that wasn't "That's What I Like About You," but in Michigan in the late eighties, you would have thought they were the Beatles.

When the curtain opened, five hundred people were expecting to see their local heroes. Then I walked out. Just one guy, talking. Before I got to my first punch line, I was being pelted with pieces of ice.

I walked off after five minutes or so, and I was met by the owner, who informed me that he wouldn't be paying me, because I didn't do my full set.

As if I were in a movie from the forties, I grabbed him by the lapels and said, "You're gonna pay me tonight, in cash, or tomorrow I'm gonna shut down this bar."

I hadn't really thought through *how* I would shut down his bar, but instead of having a bouncer throw me out on my ear, he ran to his office and counted out my money like I was on a game show.

I'd like to think that I somehow realized, instinctively, that most club owners are doing *something* shady that could get them shut down, but in the moment, I was entirely bluffing. I'm just glad he wore something with lapels.

Today, I *listen* to current artists, but I'm not likely to see them perform live. I don't want to be that weird old guy making everyone uncomfortable.

If I were at a Vampire Weekend show, I would look like a faculty advisor at a school dance. As I've gotten older, becoming part of a writhing, sweaty group of strangers has lost some of its appeal.

Some of the best live music is at festivals, but don't expect to see me at Coachella any time soon. Outdoor festivals involve some of my least favorite activities—standing, being in the sun, using a Port-a-Potty . . . Put it this way: if I'm at Bonnaroo, I'm probably in one of the medical tents with an oxygen mask.

I haven't stopped listening to new music, and you can rant all you want about how much better music was, however many years ago, but I probably won't hear you over the mix of Rhymefest and Atmosphere that I'm playing.

Again, in my mind, there is only good music and bad music. That's why my head has room for Atmosphere *and* Alabama Shakes, The Black Keys *and* Jack White, Kacey Musgraves and Charlie XCX.

I force myself to stay current with music, mostly because it tricks me into thinking I'm staying young, despite mounting physical evidence to the contrary.

A good friend of mine, who is close to my age, hasn't listened to any music that's been released since 1985, and he's been an old man since he was thirty. I think there's a connection.

My ears would love to check out new music in person. Unfortunately, they would need to bring the *rest* of my body out with them, and that's a dicey proposition.

With one bad arm, one bad leg, one bad hip, and a pesky cervical injury, I try to limit the number of times I go to places that might involve standing, or walking, or being batted around like a pinball.

So, as much as I might like to spend a couple hours in an impossibly crowded club, listening to loud, fast, angry kids play loud, fast, angry music, I'm resigned to seeing more age-appropriate fare now. I'm sure there will be a James Taylor show in my future, and that's fine. I hear he's much edgier in concert.

I've often thought it would be pretty groovy to put together a musical scrapbook with pictures and autographed CDs, but I don't *have* any pictures or autographed CDs. Luckily, I remember *something* about every concert I've seen since 1978.

My memories have some blank spots, and a few of them have become blurred together, like songs on a tape that's been recorded over too many times. Most of what I remember happened the way I remember it, but I suppose, in literature terms, I would be called an 'unreliable narrator.'

The Ramones, U.C.L.A., 1978

I wasn't 'punk' in college. I didn't own a single punk record. However, I was *aware* of punk, in the same way I was aware of London, or Mars. I had read about it, and it seemed interesting.

Since college, I've come to appreciate a lot of punk and punk-derived music. Dead Kennedys, Rage Against The Machine, and Fugazi have all, at various times, made me want to burn something to the ground, or at least send an angry tweet.

I'm a big fan of the riot grrrl sound. To me, Sleater-Kinney sound like the cool sisters I wish I would have had. I also love The Donnas, because I find them simultaneously arousing and intimidating, a combination I haven't felt since high school.

When I was *in* high school, I had yet to embrace the punk ethos, but I knew it was important. It was like when Mike Douglas booked John and Yoko on his show in '72—he might not have understood them, but he knew they meant *something*.

I needed some punk credibility, too, so in my dorm room, I tried to think of what I should wear (that may be the first time 'punk credibility' and 'dorm room' have been used in the same sentence).

I ended up wrapping my bicycle chain lock around my waist. Screw authority, I'm not wearing a normal belt!

So, I get to the venue, and the bouncer tells me I have to take the chain off. They were worried I would stage-dive and injure someone by hitting them with my midsection. I would show him.

Defiantly, I walked back to my dorm room, got the key, took off the chain, walked back to the concert, and asked the nice man to let me in. I had a great time.

I loved the purity of it. It was two hours of two-and-a-half minute songs, with no onstage banter, except the occasional "Gabba gabba hey!"

It was good to be out of my comfort zone, musically, and I could tell I was changed. In fact, when I got back to the dorm, I put on a Dan Fogelberg album, and I skipped all the ballads.

Dizzy Gillespie, U.C.L.A., 1978

This was the only other concert I saw in college, and this time I didn't try to dress for a certain look. I suppose I could have borrowed a beret from someone in the theater department, but that didn't occur to me at the time.

I knew that Dizzy Gillespie was a bandleader and a jazz trumpet player, and I knew that he played 'be-bop,' although I didn't know what that meant. I should have checked out some of his records beforehand, because I wasn't at all prepared for what I heard.

The Ramones' subject matter might not have been familiar to me, but at least they played familiar chords, arranged in a familiar structure, and in addition, they were singing.

The Gillespie band played notes in combinations I'd never heard, I couldn't always follow the structure, and nobody sang, I would get a melody line in my head, and then a whole lot of other melodies and what seemed like random notes would start happening and I'd be lost.

Since I didn't know his signature pieces at the time, I don't know what he played. I know I had a good time, but I don't know if he played "Groovin' High," or "Salt Peanuts." For as little jazz knowledge as I had at the time, the band could have been playing both of those tunes at the same time.

Strangely, what I remember most clearly was the intermission. A short time *before* intermission, in the middle (I suppose) of one tune, I had to go to the restroom.

I unobtrusively started up the aisle when the band suddenly stopped playing, and Dizzy himself then proceeded to shame me into staying until intermission.

When the lights came up, I sprinted to the restroom, motivated by a full bladder and the frenetic rhythms of be-bop. When I stepped up to . . . conduct my business, I noticed that to my right was one John Birks Gillespie. It didn't seem like a good time to introduce myself.

Jackson Browne, Riverfest (Milwaukee), 1980s (?)

I remember it was hot and muggy, and for some reason, I was walking around a music festival during the day, as opposed to when the music would be happening, which would have been at night.

At one tented stage, I saw someone at a piano in front of mostly empty bleachers. I wasn't sure who it was, but then I put the pieces together: longer-than-it-should-have-been-in-the-eighties hair, mournful voice, seemed very sensitive—it couldn't be anyone *other* than Jackson Browne.

Really, the pony-tailed guy in the front row with the 'NO NUKES' sticker on his backpack should have been my first clue. As for the small turnout, this wasn't Browne's show, but a sound check.

In a very cool gesture, he saw twenty or thirty of us who had stopped to listen, and he told us his band wouldn't be there until that night, but he would do a mini-concert by himself for us. It was like hanging out in Jackson's back yard.

Obviously I came back for the real show, since I felt like an insider at that point. Something seemed off, though. For some reason, before the show started, several event security guys positioned themselves at the front of the stage, staring at the audience with their arms folded across their chests.

There are singers whose fans are so passionate that every concert is a crowd control nightmare. There are performers who, because of their volatile lyrics, or crazy stage antics, might provoke an audience to the point of mayhem. Jackson Browne is NOT one of those performers.

Unless they were worried that his crowd would spontaneously start making protest signs, or that a few hundred people gazing at their navels was somehow a public safety risk, there was no need for DEFCON 1 security measures.

The glaring stage gargoyles were harshing our collective mellow. Admittedly, the dude in the second row shouldn't have acted on everyone's behalf by throwing an empty plastic cup at one of the security guards.

But did we need *four* of them to jump off the stage to 'subdue' this troublemaker? That's when Jackson Browne turned me into a fan for life.

He stopped in the middle of the song he was singing and said he would not continue the show until security left the stage. As he walked off, nobody knew if the show was over. Then, about fifteen minutes later, he came out with his band, all the goons had left, and he played a great show.

I wasn't a huge Jackson Browne fan before that. I owned "*The Pretender*," and maybe one other album, and "Here Come Those Tears Again" was one of my go-to songs in the shower. But after I watched him shut down 'the man' in Milwaukee, he could release an album of Justin Bieber covers and I would pay to see the tour.

Survivor / Styx / REO, L.A., 2000s

A friend took me to this as a birthday gift, I'm assuming, in order to mock me. I'm assuming this was part of their 'Past Our Prime' tour. Anyway, it's always fun to see how many of the original band members are left. I saw Foghat at a State Fair once, and I think it was the drummer and three guys who *owned* Foghat albums.

The opening act was Survivor who proved they were aptly named by showing up, and as a bonus, they did that one song they were known for. They may have done several other songs, as well.

Nobody in the crowd seemed to be there *for* Survivor, but their part of the show gave me time to think about which Styx songs I wanted to hear.

I would call my love for Styx a guilty pleasure, except that I'm remarkably guilt-free about it. With my background and wiring, how could I not be into a band whose lead singer sang rock songs like they were Broadway show-stoppers?

Unfortunately, when I saw them, Dennis DeYoung was not the lead singer of Styx anymore, but the guy who replaced him was adequately theatrical. To their credit, this incarnation of the band ridiculed, instead of playing, their unfortunate 1983 hit, "Mr. Roboto."

By the time of their encore, "Renegade," fifteen hundred middle-aged, paunchy, balding white men were on their feet. I could have been at the Republican National Convention, if not for all the Bic lighters in the air.

On this tour, Styx and REO Speedwagon alternated the 'headline' spot on the bill between them, which meant that half the time, (including the show I saw), the closing act was REO.

Of all the lineups that have been booked on concert stages, this was one of the most wrongheaded, like Hendrix opening for The Monkees, and Prince warming up the crowd for The Stones. Ideally, a rock concert should have momentum, with the energy and volume building to a climax.

When REO followed Styx, you went from big guitars and fist-pumping celebrations of triumph to a few piano chords and a thin, wimpy voice singing,

> *Heard it from a friend who*
>
> *Heard it from a friend who*
>
> *Heard it from another you've been messin' around.*

I'm sure they *eventually* rocked, a bit, but I have no idea how REO closed their set, because I had joined the ranks of my brethren heading to the exits, trying not to think about how little any of us rocked anymore.

For the other concerts I've seen, my memories are scattershot at best. I don't remember years, or venues, or setlists. At some shows, I don't even know who was with me. Looking back now, I wish I had kept a few pictures, asked for a few autographs, or at the very least, kept a few ticket stubs.

Brave Combo

Seeing this show allowed me to check off the boxes for 'polka,' 'cha-cha.' 'norteño,' 'ska,' 'salsa' and 'merengue' on my Genres Seen In Concert checklist.

Their founder, Carl Finch, once said "I felt like being in a polka band was about the most punk thing we could do," and short of wearing a bike lock as a belt, I would agree.

Nanci Griffith

I've never bought into traditional symbols of religion, and my theology is complicated. That being said, if there is a God, *and* if there is a Heaven, *and* if that Heaven includes clouds, *and* if those clouds contain angels, *AND if those angels sing,* I believe they will sound like Nancy Griffith.

k.d. lang

Great voice, amazing range, and *very* devoted fans. The crowd response made it feel like I was watching Elvis, if Elvis had been a vegan, Buddhist, LGBT activist working for human rights in Tibet.

Sandra Bernhard

Another sound check story: Bernhard is as idiosyncratic a singer as she is a comedian, and I happened to catch a rehearsal of her slow burn through Prince's "Little Red Corvette," with nobody else around, before an outdoor festival show.

I went to the 'backstage' area and told her she reminded me of Laura Nyro, and she told me Nyro was a musical higher power for her. We didn't meet *per se*, but I thought we bonded.

Frank Sinatra, Jr.

When I saw Frank Jr. in Vegas, I felt bad for the guy. We're at the Desert Inn, a place his father single-handedly put on the map, but *Junior's* show isn't in the main showroom, it's on a stage in the middle of a slot machine pit. And it was *free*.

It makes me sad, because the show was main room quality, and at least worth twenty bucks. His band swung hard, and his voice was at least as good as his father's was at the same age.

I couldn't put my finger on what was missing, but my girlfriend at the time nailed it: "He's like his dad, but without the charisma." Still, he felt closer to the real thing than any number of Rat Pack pretenders working today.

Chuck E. Weiss

A friend of mine is plugged into a lot of very funky and intimate venues, which fits, because he's a huge fan of the blues. I've always thought the blues are best heard in a venue where you can get close to the suffering, where you can really feel the sweat and tears.

As opposed to a massive outdoor blues festival, where you might miss the headliner, because you're stuck in line buying another strip of tickets so that you can get one more eleven dollar beer.

So, in a tiny L.A. club, I saw Chuck E. Weiss. Now, I only knew about him from reading about Tom Waits, with whom he lived at the Tropicana, and listening to Rickie Lee Jones ("Chuck E's In Love"). At the time, I did *not* know that he had played with Lightnin' Hopkins, Muddy Waters, and Howlin' Wolf.

Admittedly, I wasn't raised with the blues, but I'm pretty sure that if you've been onstage with three people who, instead of their first names, are known as 'Lightnin',' Howlin',' and 'Muddy,' you probably have legitimate blues chops. Chuck E. is authentic.

Peter Wolf

The other end of the Blues Veracity Spectrum would be the loosely-named House of Blues. First, being a chain, it's already about seventeen steps removed from anything that's genuinely 'bluesy.'

Then there's the fact that the two people most identified with the club are pretend bluesman Dan Aykroyd and the inexplicably famous Jim Belushi.

Good rule of thumb: if a joint sells 'Portobello sliders' and 'Caprese salad,' it's probably not the real deal. Or you can check their calendar. Not for nothing, but this means I went to the L.A. House of 'Blues' twice, and heard no blues.

First, I saw Peter Wolf, who fronted the J. Geils Band, which was briefly known as the J. Geils *Blues* Band. However, they dropped the 'blues,' and most people only know them for a few MTV and radio hits.

This time, he was performing without them, effectively severing any connection he might have had to the blues. Prokofiev's "Peter AND the Wolf'" would have been bluesier than this guy singing "*Centerfold.*"

Henry Rollins

This 'show' was not only blues-free, it was *music*-free as well. Mr. Rollins is in my concert scrapbook because, when I went, I was expecting music.

Rollins famously became lead vocalist for Los Angeles punk band Black Flag, and later performed spoken word shows, so I was primed for a night of screaming, raw poetry with a punk attitude. At the House of 'Blues,' so I should have known better.

In this case, the 'show' I caught happened after he became known for Gap ads, Learning Channel shows, and the film *Jackass Number Two.*

His entire performance consisted mostly of stories about hanging with celebrities on movie sets. It was like a live, khakis-clad, muscle-bound version of '*Entertainment Tonight.*'

Three Random Bands (and a knife fight)

From the sixties through the eighties, the Sunset Strip was the center of the Los Angeles rock scene, and Gazzarri's, along with the Rainbow and the Roxy, was ground zero.

Van Halen was a featured house band there, before Eddie got sober and Diamond Dave got fat, and then got skinny again. Gazzarri's featured acts ranging from Tina Turner to Ratt, and from The Doors to Guns N' Roses.

It was the epicenter of the glam metal scene, and it was even featured in a Huey Lewis video, although that's probably more of a negative. Regardless, I knew that, though I wasn't a rocker (or glam, for that matter), I needed to experience the place.

The night I went, nobody famous was on the bill, and I don't think anybody I heard *became* famous. There was however, a palpable, sweaty, crazy energy in the place, with a whiff of rock and roll desperation, and it was heady stuff. Oh, and there was a knife fight.

Gazzarri's had three stages for live music, and I had wandered upstairs, when suddenly I heard yelling, and I saw people in the crowd scuffling and pushing each other.

From what I recall, one woman had a knife and was screaming at another woman, and then somebody knocked the knife from her hand to the ground, and somebody kicked the knife away. All in all, it was a good show.

Aerosmith

Seeing a legendary arena-rock band in an intimate venue in their home town is amazing. I consider myself lucky enough to have seen Aerosmith in a small Boston bar.

The only downside to the show was the fact that, at the time I was in Boston, I was toggling between an out-of-control gambling problem and excessive drinking, so there's a *slight* possibility that I only *imagined* seeing Aerosmith.

Ladysmith Black Mambazo

It was Minneapolis, and it was winter, because, when isn't it winter in Minneapolis? Anyway, try to imagine eight Zulu performers from South Africa performing on a symphonic concert stage in one of the whitest cities in the United States.

Then picture just over two thousand Minnesotans filled with something that approximated joy, and this was a foot-stomping, whooping and hollering version of joy, not the muted, Scandinavian "it's finally above freezing" type of joy Minnesotans usually feel.

Stevie Wonder

I suppose the world's largest food festival isn't where you would expect to see one of the world's greatest singer-songwriters. Yet there was Stevie Wonder, in front of a huge crowd spread out on the grass.

Everybody seemed to have a good time, but the crowd's energy felt off. The vibe was subdued, and not as boisterous as the music we were hearing. It's almost as if hours of walking in oppressive heat and humidity while gorging on fried foods makes people less energetic.

I don't recall many specifics, because when I went to Taste of Chicago in 2008, I found myself in yet another new city, broke (again), and trying to figure out a way to stay afloat.

Most of the time I spent in Chicago was a blur. But for part of an afternoon, I was given a break from the grind and was transported to "Higher Ground."

Gary Puckett

I have a friend who loves the Minnesota State Fair with the wide-eyed enthusiasm of an eight-year-old boy at Christmas in a Norman Rockwell painting. He is the least cynical person I have ever met.

Strange, then, that he asked *me* to spend a day with him at the 'Great Minnesota Get-Together,' knowing that I might, at any moment, go off the rails and flip out before we got our first walleye-on-a-stick.

This friend is so enamored of the Fair that he arrives before the fairgrounds open, because we wouldn't want to miss the dog-jumping show, and we certainly wouldn't want to be rushed in the butter sculpture pavilion.

Thankfully for him, we got high in the parking lot beforehand, but it wasn't enough to prevent me from alternating between being bored and being annoyed. I was not in the right mindset for all the walking, standing, and sweating, and I became wee bit whiny.

Thankfully for me, my friend's love of heartland celebration must have been stronger than his desire to leave my whiny ass there, because he stayed with me long enough for us to enjoy some music.

First, we saw Gary Puckett (without the Union Gap) and it was like most shows on the 'oldies' circuit—an old guy singing old songs with backing musicians that could have been his children. It was like watching somebody's fairly cool dad sing karaoke.

He was still in good voice, but I had trouble getting past the songs themselves. Not a wide range of subjects: "Woman, Woman," "Lady Willpower," "This Girl Is A Woman Now," and most disturbingly, "Young Girl." Sure, the late sixties was a different era, but didn't *anybody* think these songs were creepy?

Los Lobos

At that same state fair, for a magical hour or so, I stopped complaining, my friend stopped being bothered by my complaining, and all was forgiven. That's because we got to sit down in the shade and watch one of the most criminally unheralded bands of the last thirty years.

It's a shame that Los Lobos is only familiar to casual listeners for their cover of Ritchie Valens' "La Bamba," because they have a music legacy that reaches far beyond the soundtrack to a Lou Diamond Phillips movie.

Active and musically relevant since the early seventies, Los Lobos incorporates Tex-Mex, country, folk, R&B, blues, soul, cumbia, boleros, norteños and rock into a tasty stew, flavored by tangy guitar leads and "cry in your *cerveza*" vocals.

They are the only band I've seen live who can jump from *norteamericano* roots music to experimental soundscapes in the same set. If that isn't enough, in '09 they released *Los Lobos Goes Disney,* which includes a killer version of "I Wanna Be Like You," from *The Jungle Book.*

Wayne Newton

I'll admit to a fondness for Vegas schlock. It must, however, achieve a *level* of schlock that transcends simple cheese and easy camp. If you have the chutzpah to steal a page from Sinatra's book, you can't be lazy about it. Michael Bublé tries to get there, but to my ears, he's not even *faux* Frank, he's *faux* Frank Jr.

If you want real deal schmaltz, you need someone who has immersed himself in smarmy clichés for so long that schmaltz is part of his DNA. You need to go to a Wayne Newton show.

At some point in the mid-eighties, I found myself doing standup at a place called the Carleton Celebrity Room in Minneapolis. The comics played the 'Backstage' room there, and the main room was home to the big name musical acts.

One night between shows, I wandered into the main room for the start of Wayne Newton's show. I could only stay for the first song, but that one number contained enough over-the-top showbiz clichés to save me a dozen trips to Las Vegas.

First of all, the song he opened with was Neil Diamond's "America," which somehow manages to combine simplistic nostalgia and knee-jerk patriotism with Brill Building hooks and rhinestone glitz.

There were symphonic crescendos, flashing lights, and there may well have been a fog machine. Then, there was the entrance of The Wayne, who, in the span of ten minutes, managed to play guitar, violin, and trumpet solos while belting lyrics about home, and dreams, and freedom.

It was ridiculously excessive, like a Fourth of July episode of *H.R. Pufnstuf,* and *the crowd loved it.* Wayne Newton *was* "coming to America," dammit, and America (represented by the audience) had no choice but to embrace him. It was also refreshing, because there was nothing arch or ironic about it.

There was just an inexplicable sincerity that was light-years removed from the self-consciously smug mentality of some contemporary acts.

I left the showroom feeling like I had just bought a car I didn't need from a salesman I didn't like, all because the test drive was so much fun.

Tony Bennett

I saw Tony Bennett at the same venue where I saw Wayne Newton's extravaganzapalooza, and this time I stayed for the whole show. Before the show, I didn't have a strong opinion about Tony Bennett.

To me, he represented my mom's music. He even grew up in Astoria in Queens, where Mom was born. Although a couple of promos for him on MTV caught my attention, I was inclined to dismiss him as another purveyor of dusty old 'classics.'

It didn't take more than a few songs for me to get caught up in the literal swing of things. Here was a guy taking songs, none of which he wrote, and *interpreting* them. It was like he was acting *while* he was singing!

Having grown up in an era that canonized the singer-songwriter and marginalized singers who *only* sang, this was a strange concept to me.

He changed rhythms, he toyed with phrasing, and he seemed to be connected to the lyrics in a way that made it feel like he *created* the words he was singing right there in the moment. It was as if he found some abandoned property, saw it had potential, and decided to build a home there.

One gesture from his show sealed it for me, and turned me into a Bennett fan for life. Late in the show, for the obligatory encore, he sang his signature tune, "I Left My Heart In San Francisco."

When he got to the line, "your golden sun will shine on me," on the word 'sun,' he put one hand up as if to shield his eyes from the sun.

From a less committed artist, it would have been laughably cheesy. From Tony, everyone there bought it. He believed it, so we believed it, and sometimes art is as simple as that.

Sinatra once said, "*For my money, Tony Bennett is the best singer in the business*," and that quote illustrates one of the fundamental rules of entertainment—never argue with Frank.

The Sincerest Form of Flattery

There is quite a difference between enjoying a musical artist and being a fan, and I've never had that 'fanatic' piece. I can't see being devoted to a band, and besides that, I have the attention span of a five-year old, so I would never be able to focus my fan energy on one group.

Every music act has superfans, the type of people who devote most of their free time and all of their disposable income to following 'their' musical lodestone. In the case of the Grateful Dead, the fan component and the fan *experience* is as important as the music.

You start to realize that the music is secondary to the event if you've ever known a Deadhead. At some point, that Deadhead will force you to listen to a fifty-two-minute jam that starts out as "Sugar Magnolia" but ends up sounding like a cross between a drum circle and a hootenanny. In space.

The journeys of Deadheads have been well-chronicled, but every band has that group of people who were there from the beginning. These are the people who believe that 'their' band somehow has an obligation to constantly perform and at the same time, never change how they sound.

I've never felt that same sense of *loyalty* to a performer. For artists I respect, I'll listen to anything they release, but if they take a creative turn that leaves me cold, I don't feel like they've violated some sacred trust. I just don't buy that album, and I wait to hear what the next one sounds like.

I think I'm still feeling burned from that time in my teens when Hamilton, Joe Frank, and Reynolds suddenly became Hamilton, Joe Frank and *Dennison*.

One day, I'm in the soft-rock aisle of my local record store, looking for the follow-up to *Fallin' In Love*, and Reynolds was just gone.

So, though I have great faith in music, I'm not as inclined to have much faith in musicians. I probably know as much about Bob Dylan as a hardcore Dylan 'fan,' but I'm not following him from city to city on tour, or spending thousands of dollars on rare acetates of third takes of unreleased bootleg tracks.

Musicians, like people in general, sometimes let you down. Some of the people who made powerful music with Jefferson Airplane went on to make horrifyingly bad music with Starship. Then again, most of us made regrettable choices in the eighties.

It's not that I don't appreciate artists who are evolving. Following your muse can lead to great art, but not every experiment is worth pursuing, or more accurately, worth recording and asking your fans to buy. I'm looking at you, Neil Young, and your strange techno album. Put down the vocoder and grab your guitar. You're good at the guitar.

Unfortunately, some music fans, especially the ones who have followed an artist since 'before they got huge,' think that those musicians must, in perpetuity, always sound exactly like they did 'back in the day.'

"You should have heard them on their first tour, man! They were so raw, they could barely play their instruments!" Gee, maybe over the years, they've learned to play better! Maybe they can afford better equipment. Are they supposed to deliberately suck again so that you can relive your youth?

When REM were college radio darlings, a lot of critics praised their lyrics. I always thought they had a cool sound, but on their early albums, Michael Stipe's vocals were so mumbled that he could have been singing the words to a supermarket flyer, for all I could tell.

Also, the 'sellout' label is thrown around too loosely for my taste. Sure, you might be annoyed that some band you think you and your three bros *discovered* has a big radio hit, and it's frustrating when you find out they're playing arenas larger than your basement apartment.

On the other hand, it's entirely possible that your underground heroes actually *intended* to sell their records, become popular, and make money at their career, so that they didn't have to play dive bars anymore!

One of the most specious criticisms musicians hear is that they are too 'commercial.' Understand, I'm not talking about genuine examples of pandering to mainstream taste. If Rage Against the Machine reunited to record a bunch of One Direction songs, *that* would be selling out.

However, *selling* your music is not the same as selling *out*, and for most musical entities, the idea from the beginning was to *sell* their art. To continue making art and distributing it to their fans, artists frequently need money.

There are not many musicians who, at the start, are thinking, "I have to make sure I don't make too much money, so that my girlfriend will have to keep driving me to crappy gigs, and so that the ten people who see me at those gigs don't think I've sold out."

For a lot of working musicians, before they get the *chance* to compromise their integrity with their own songs, they were paying the bills playing songs made famous by other people. 'Cover bands' have created a storied legacy, from bar mitzvahs, proms, and weddings to conventions, cruise ships and casino lounges.

In that sense, cover bands have probably provided the soundtrack to at least one of the major events in your life, whether it's been coming of age, high school graduation, professing your love, taking a vacation, or becoming a compulsive gambler.

If someone has heard "Born To Be Wild" in person, it is statistically more likely that they heard it performed by a band named something like 'Rock 'n Roll Magick' or 'The Oldies Machine' than by Steppenwolf.

In my experience in the comedy scene, there was no equivalent to the 'cover band.' There were no 'cover comics,' because if you were doing someone else's joke, it was called stealing. Audiences got this, although I did have somebody ask me after a show once if I "did any Robin Williams."

I don't dispute that the majority of cover bands playing the hotel circuit are profoundly mediocre, but I don't have a problem with the *concept* of cover bands.

For me, they serve two purposes. First, it's not like your reunion committee could afford to hire *real* eighties bands to play at your 'New Wave Dance Night', and secondly, they allow musicians to pay their rent.

Before the rock era, there were singers, and there were songwriters. This was primarily because there are different skill sets involved. The Gershwins didn't try to sing, and Frank Sinatra didn't try to write. Most songwriters from the era of the 'Great American Songbook' were, at best, mediocre singers.

The mindset changed with the advent of the singer-songwriter. Songwriters' voices weren't necessarily any better, but by the seventies, if you wrote songs, it became the norm to record them yourself.

The rise of the singer-songwriter gave fans the idea that, if you 'only' sang, you were somehow less talented than if you played three chords on the guitar, owned a rhyming dictionary, and *also* sang.

I'm oversimplifying there, but no more so than people who dismiss vocalists who 'don't write their own songs.' *Interpreting* a lyric can be as creative and revelatory as writing one. Check out Johnny Winter's furious, primal slide-guitar version of Dylan's "Highway 61" if you don't believe me.

Cover bands deserve some slack, because everybody is in on the scam. We know it's not really Creedence doing that Creedence tune, and the musicians know that they're not really Creedence. Everyone agrees to play along.

If you want to take your pretending to the next level, there are 'tribute acts.' The difference between a cover act and a *tribute* act is the level of commitment. In most cases, the guy singing Simon LeBon's part in a cover band isn't trying to convince anyone that he is actually Simon Le Bon.

Elvis Presley impersonators represent a different, and sometimes creepier, experience. I always felt that if Elvis hadn't died, he might have resurfaced as an Elvis impersonator. He could play state fairs and Ramada Inns, and his cover would be safe, because nobody would think it was *really* Elvis in the Ramada Inn bar.

The only time I worked with a tribute act was on a one-nighter in Osakis, Minnesota. They were a Blues Brothers tribute act. They were also very committed to their roles, driving to the gig in a replica Bluesmobile.

Their show was entertaining, and 'Jake' and 'Elwood' gave the banquet crowd far more energy than they got back. It was almost surreal to watch, though—two white Minnesotans doing an impression of two fictional characters created by two other white guys who were paying tribute to the blues. The music might have lost a little along the way.

Then again, how many of those people in Osakis, Minnesota, had ever connected with *any* blues music before seeing this show?

As far as I'm concerned, those guys did a public service. If they convinced even a few people in the middle of the tundra to listen to some Junior Wells or Big Joe Turner, then they *were* 'on a mission from God.'

It's taken me all my life to learn what not to play.

--Dizzy Gillespie

Word Problems

As much as I love to sing, and as much as I love listening to singers, there are times when I don't want my music served with a side order of words.

Sometimes, the words are so distractingly bad, that I get knocked clear out of the song and start questioning whether I like music at all.

It usually happens when I'm singing along to something. I'm immersed in my own personal karaoke booth, when I'll sing a line and catch myself, because the words I'm singing sound stupid. I notice it because I'm the one singing.

This all may seem obvious, but I can't count the number of times I've been in a car with someone singing along, pointed out a bad lyric, and had that person respond with, "Oh, I never really paid attention to the words." How can that be? *You're* singing them!

The first time a song lyric threw me out of a song, I was deep into my Carole King phase. Unlike most red-blooded teenage boys, I was engrossed in the *Tapestry* album.

Of course, this was during ancient times, so I was listening to the songs in a preset order determined by the artist and a mysterious presence known as the 'record label.'

So, I'm relating to each lyric and feeling like Carole King is singing to me *personally*. Then in the middle of an otherwise solid tune called "Home Again," one of the most respected pop songwriters of the sixties and seventies sings this line: *'Snow is cold, rain is wet. Chills my soul right to the marrow.'*

I could never really trust Carole King after that. I want to believe that she was saying that *bad lyrics* like 'snow is cold, rain is wet' are what chills her soul, but I have a feeling Carole just couldn't think of any metaphors that day.

Frankly, it's the same with Carole King's PBS pledge week buddy, James Taylor. I love every corny, syrupy, corn syrupy vocal tic of his, and I have dozens of his songs in my phone.

But I can't listen to his early song, "Long Ago and Far Away" anymore—not after the first time I heard him sing, '*Love is just a word I heard when things were being said.*' Well, at least you heard it when things were being said, because otherwise you were hallucinating.

If I really enjoy a song, I can listen past a clunker of a phrase, gritting my teeth and maybe twitching a little when I hear it.

I seem to always reach a point, though, when that one, small piece of lazy lyric writing becomes bigger than the song itself, and that clunker becomes all I can hear.

I don't think you need to be a licensed grammarian to spot the incorrect word choice in the Neil Diamond classic, "Play Me," but consider this a trigger warning anyway--

Song she sang to me

Song she <u>brang</u> to me

Words that rang in me,

Rhyme that sprang from me

Kudos for finding three words that rhyme with 'sang,' but I'm afraid the judges cannot accept 'brang,' *because it's not a word!*

Are you telling me nobody in the studio at the time, not one of the engineers, not a single musician playing on the track—*nobody* called Neil on that one?

It wouldn't be so painful if it weren't for Neil Diamond's vocal style. Never known for his understated delivery, in this one he hits '*brang*' so hard it's as if he's trying to *convince* you it's a real word with sheer force of will.

It's one thing to be nondescript, or obtuse, and I can even tolerate the occasional cliché. You lose me when you *stack* the clichés on top of each other, creating a sort of monument to hackneyed sentiment.

Individually, both Lionel Richie and Kenny Rogers have made enough good music to be forgiven for some of the mind-numbing pabulum they've created. Kenny very nearly rocked when he was with the First Edition, and the Commodores allowed large numbers of white people to feel funky.

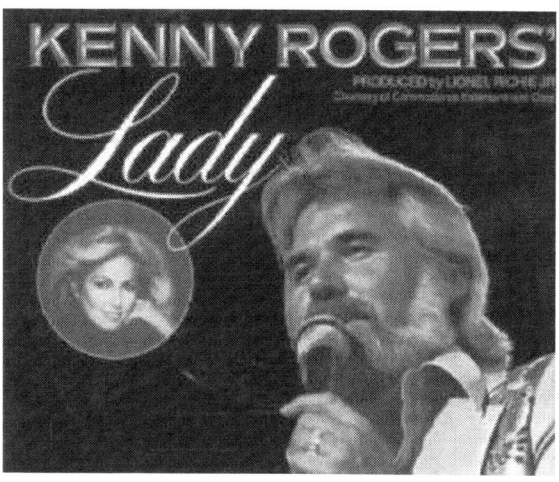

Combine these two Exemplars of Bland and you get something so mushy it makes the Carpenters seem like the White Stripes. However, as justified as it would be to haul Kenny Rogers before a music tribunal for punishment, Lionel Richie is responsible for 'writing' the words to "Lady" . . .

> *Lady, I'm your knight in shining armor, and I love you.*
>
> *You have made me what I am, and I am yours.*
>
> *My love, there's so many ways I want to say I love you.*
>
> *Let me hold you in my arms forever more.*

For those of you scoring at home, that would be six clichés in the span of four lines. The only part of the verse that is less cliché is when he mentions that there are 'so many ways' to say 'I love you.' Apparently, he couldn't think of any *original* ones when he was writing this song.

My nitpicking, as some might call it, has even ruined a classic holiday song, but oddly enough, not until years after I first heard it. Since I was a boy, I have been singing the Andy Williams versions of all the traditional carols.

I've also been fond of his more secular Christmas hit, "It's The Most Wonderful Time Of The Year." It's the musical equivalent of a Christmas sweater—it might be tacky, but it's warm. To say nothing of the fact that the horn section swings pretty hard.

Unfortunately, when Andy gets to the song's bridge, he is forced to sing a line that, in a Christmas song, is at once confusing and disturbing:

There'll be scary ghost stories and tales of the glories of--

Wait--what was that line right before the whole 'tales of glories' part? *Scary ghost stories*? What kind of hellish Dickensian childhood did you have? Who tells ghost stories at Christmas? "Get over here by the tree, kids! Time for stories about dead people!"

I really wish I *didn't* notice the words to songs as much as I do, but I can't switch that off. What makes *that* a problem is that I have a savant-like ability to *remember* song lyrics.

I'm a pub trivia god, if the category happens to be 'Songs That Were On The Radio Between 1970 and 1990.' If you say the title of a song that was popular during those twenty years, I can tell you the lyrics. I'll most likely sing them to you.

When it comes to song *titles*, as a rule, they should tell us what the song is about, or evoke some sort of emotion that will be tapped when we hear the song. When you just take some random words and slap them on top of the music, you're not being clever, you're being annoying.

A good example of a functional title is Johnny Mercer's "Drinking Again." It clearly tells you what the song is about, which is somebody drinking.

Again. Compare this straightforward approach to that of Bob Dylan, who wrote a song that should have been called "I Hate You, Go Away," but ended up with the title "Positively 4th Street."

Song titles themselves can be deal breakers for me, and I'm not always rational about it. I hate the Smashing Pumpkins tune, "Mayonnaise," entirely because it's a ridiculous title. The song is not *about* mayonnaise, nor does mayonnaise *represent* anything in the song.

Titles with parenthetical phrases bother me more than they should. A lot of parentheticals seem defensive. "Escape (The Pina Colada Song)" is basically songwriter Rupert Holmes acknowledging that the only thing memorable *about* the song is the titular drink.

> *"Fine. You can call it 'The Pina Colada Song.' But it should be called 'Escape,' because it tells a story, you know."*

Sometimes, writers seem to add parentheses because they're worried we won't get the twist. "Dude (Looks Like A Lady)" should have just been titled, "Dude," so that the fact that he '(Looks Like a Lady)' would be a surprise. That's basic storytelling. Although it was 1987, so Aerosmith probably felt a need to clear that part up right away.

A few other problematic parentheticals:

"P.Y.T. (Pretty Young Thing)"—
The thing about an abbreviation is, if you have to tell us what it means, the abbreviation is pointless.

"Movin' Out (Anthony's Song)"—

We can figure out that it's 'Anthony's song,' because Billy Joel says his name in the first line.

"The 59ᵗʰ St. Bridge Song (Feelin' Groovy)"—

I'm sure Art Garfunkel had to lobby Paul Simon for the parentheses here, explaining that the 59th Street Bridge only means something in New York, so he might want to include the rest of us.

"I Believe (When I Fall In Love It Will Be Forever)"—

Nobody was going to tell Stevie Wonder that his title's too long, but it is. Why not put all the lyrics in the title?

"It's The End Of The World As We Know It (And I Feel Fine)"—

Also too long, but it is somehow comforting to know that Michael Stipe feels fine.

"I'm Always Touched By Your (Presence Dear)"—
Here's an interesting case wherein neither the title nor the parenthetical makes sense by itself. Punctuation tip: if you need what's inside the curvy lines to make sense of what's *outside* the curvy lines, think of a new title.

"Shoop Shoop" has been both inside parenthesis, after "Exhale," and outside, before "It's In His Kiss." To my knowledge, no song has ever been released called "(Shoop Shoop) Shoop Shoop," but if there were it would be a huge hit.

One of the worst titles of a popular song from the past fifty years is B. J. Thomas' "(Hey, Won't You Play) Another Somebody Done Somebody Wrong Song?"

First, "Another Somebody Done Somebody Wrong Song" would be too long *without* the parentheses. Then you've got parentheses, plus a comma, and a question mark, it's got bad grammar AND it finds a way to combine two clichés! Pleasant enough song, though.

Incredibly, *"(Hey, Won't You Play)"* is not the longest title in the history of the Billboard Charts. That honor goes to a truly execrable song crime committed by a group of Dutch singers known as Stars on 45.

In 1981, they cobbled together a medley of ten hit songs, performed *approximately* like the original versions.

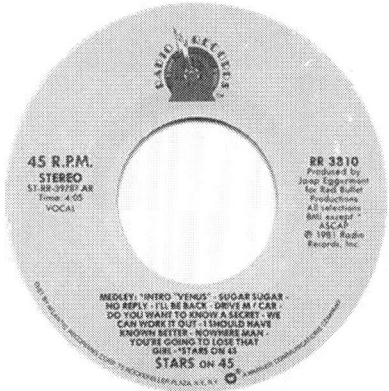

Almost no attention is paid to matching tempos, or logical segues, or the fact that for some reason it's eight Beatles songs, an Archies song, and the song "Venus." Then, clearly exhausted from watering down all that good music, they don't even try to come up with a decent title.

The title of this Number One hit record, the longest title for a Billboard chart single in the rock era, a title as bereft of creativity *and* imagination as the medley itself:

> "Intro Venus/Sugar Sugar/No Reply/I'll Be Back/Drive My Car/Do You Want to Know a Secret/We Can Work It Out/I Should Have Known Better/You're Going to Lose That Girl/Stars on 45"

I have a suggestion for any fledgling songwriters reading this book. If you can't think of what to call a song, don't do what painters do—don't call it "Untitled." You're a writer—you can write a few more words and come up with a title. And whatever you do, (try to avoid using) parentheses.

And the Nominees Aren't . . .

I'm a sucker for award shows. If the National Association of Public Insurance Adjusters gave out awards, and they televised a handful of famous public insurance adjusters giving out those awards on a big stage with a curtain, I would watch.

I've never thought the Grammys represented the *best* in music. But despite the outrageous omissions and ridiculous nominations, I try to catch the Grammys every year.

That's because there's always one supremely awkward moment that makes the tedious speeches and bloated production numbers worthwhile.

One year, I could swear I watched Rosemary Clooney present an award with Kid Rock. In addition, the hosting always feels forced and stilted, lately with L.L. Cool J desperately trying to remind viewers that he, too, used to be in the music business.

The first host of the Grammys was political comic Mort Sahl in 1959, which was coincidentally the last time the Grammys had any edge.

The awards weren't televised until 1971, a year when John and Yoko jammed with Zappa, the Allman Brothers recorded a classic live album, and Deep Purple got the inspiration for "Smoke on the Water."

So naturally, the National Academy of Recording Arts and Sciences in 1971 chose Andy Williams to host the first televised Grammy Awards. I've always felt a special connection to the music of Andy Williams, but even my eleven-year old self thought he was an odd choice.

Yet the Grammys, in a steadfast effort to avoid being current, stuck with their choice for the next seven years. The seventies were the decade that gave us punk, disco, and new wave, yet music's biggest celebration for most of that decade was hosted by the guy who recorded "Moon River" in 1961.

The Academy finally made a change in 1978, a year that brought us first albums by Van Halen and the Dead Kennedys, and The Who's last album with Keith Moon. It only makes sense, that the host of the 1978 Grammy Awards was John Denver.

The most incongruous moment of those seventies Grammy shows was always the medley of each year's Song of the Year nominees. As a general rule, I think medleys are a bad idea, whether you're talking about songs or frozen vegetables.

Anyway, instead of the nominated artists performing their songs, the host would do about thirty seconds of each one. That doesn't sound like much, but when it's John Denver gamely trying to sell "Hotel California," thirty seconds is more than enough.

The area of Grammy oversights and boneheaded choices is well-trod ground. One year, Jethro freaking *Tull* won Best Hard Rock / Metal Performance. A Taste of Honey took Best New Artist from Elvis Costello.

It's clear that Grammy voters don't have a clue who should win in most categories. Just ask 1981's Best New Artist, Christopher Cross. He hasn't had an album on the U.S. charts since 1984, so he's probably free if you want to hang with him.

The saddest thing is that the Grammys don't even know which *categories* are important. The Recording Academy lost me entirely in 2009, when they decided to eliminate the category of Best Polka Recording.

In an egregious miscarriage of justice and an insult to good, right-thinking Americans, the Academy released a statement that polka had been eliminated to "ensure the awards process remains representative of the current musical landscape." Well, there's a Grammy for Best Spoken Word Recording, and I defy you to try dancing to any of the winners in *that* category.

There was also some nonsense in the Academy's statement about 'relevance,' but I don't buy any of it. The voting members of the record industry care about relevance about as much as a Kardashian cares about privacy. Regardless of the rationale, the world is a sadder place with less polka in it.

distraught Polka-Americans react to Grammy snub

This is a form of musical expression which has touched us all. Whether you've danced with a drunk aunt at a Wisconsin wedding (*like I'm the only one*) or simply lounged around your apartment in a new pair of lederhosen (*just me, again?*), you can't deny the power of the oom-pah-pah.

The Academy in its wisdom has decided the polka is no longer 'relevant.' In a country which celebrates diversity, this is a slap in the face with a raw bratwurst. No Grammy for polka music? That's like not having a Nobel Prize for...polka music.

Now, tragically, polka music has been absorbed into the 'Regional Roots Music' category, where it has to share the spotlight with Cajun, Hawaiian, Native American, and zydeco music, because they all sound the same, right? Please.

And what's next? First, it's no polka award, then maybe they stop giving away awards for jazz . . . then classical is dismissed . . . then rock. Soon, the Grammy Awards show becomes three and a half hours of Ariana Grande.

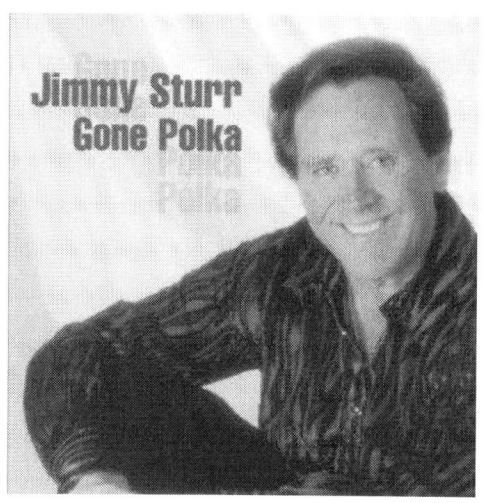

Jimmy Sturr has received more Grammys, with eighteen, than Bruce Springsteen. That's eighteen of the twenty-four awards *ever* given for Best Polka Album.

Yet when asked by the New York Times about his success, Sturr was humble: *"I'm not going to say I'm the best band in the whole world, but we're just as good as any."*

True enough. But what of the dozens of fresh-faced kids who begged their daddies for their first used accordions? To what can *they* aspire? They won't be able to break Jimmy's polka Grammy record, because there won't be any more polka Grammys to receive.

To be sure, polka has its critics. Some people claim that polka music leads to alcoholism, while others believe that alcohol leads to polka music. Despite these concerns, one thing is clear—polka music deserves to be celebrated as much as any other genre.

When asked about the popularity of polka music as compared to other, more 'award-worthy' genres, once again Jimmy Sturr put it best when he told *The Times*, *"Polka isn't the biggest,"* he said, *"but it's not the smallest, either."* How true, Jimmy. How very true.

"Music is, to me, proof of the existence of God.
It is so extraordinarily full of magic."

--Kurt Vonnegut

Scary Music

I'll freely admit that some of the music I enjoy is filed under 'easy listening.' At the same time, I realize that term has some negative connotations, but I'm fine with it.

I don't always *want* 'hard listening,' any more than I always want 'hard liquor.' Sometimes I *want* music that goes down easy, and doesn't make my head hurt.

I have friends who claim that they enjoy 'all kinds of music,' but when pressed, there's always an exception. "I listen to everything except rap," or, "I like all music except country." For some of my friends, the exception is classical music.

For many contemporary music fans, the only thing they know about the symphonic world is that Beethoven was deaf, a fact that makes me think that he might have been the first person to yell to a concert crowd, "I can't hear you!" There is, however, more to classical music than that.

I've always believed that music genres were fairly meaningless distinctions, but I suppose they can be useful.

For instance, if you're writing a book about music, and most of your reference points are from popular music, and then you want to write about music that *isn't* so popular, you need to call that other music *something*.

The phrase 'unpopular music,' while possibly accurate, is too off-putting. I can't imagine a classical music station advertising itself as "your radio home for unpopular music."

In common parlance, 'classical' music is used for everything from huge symphonic orchestral pieces to pieces for solo bassoon, so that's not helpful at all. To add to the confusion, the period in 'classical music' from about 1750 to 1820 is called the 'Classical' period.

The term 'serious music' gets tossed around by critics, but that implies that a lot of great music isn't 'serious,' so that's just snobbery. Some critics use the phrase 'art music,' which makes about as much sense as 'furniture chairs' or 'vehicular cars.'

Maybe music genres should reflect accessibility. We already have 'comfort food,' so why not 'comfort music?' Which would make what the New York Philharmonic plays 'gourmet music,' I suppose.

Since not everyone has adopted *my* system of music taxonomy, wherein music is either Good or Bad, I need to find a term for what is usually called 'classical music.' It should be something that readily identifies that music as being different than rock or jazz.

Then I realized that, unlike the audience for a rock band or a jazz ensemble, when most people go to the symphony or a recital hall, they dress nicer, and frequently, the musicians dress up, too, so I've decided to call the music you hear in those places 'fancy music.'

I had the opportunity to see the Saint Paul Chamber Orchestra perform their fancy music in a church sanctuary (extra fancy!), and I've heard the Chicago Symphony Orchestra perform in their exceedingly fancy concert hall.

Watching an orchestra play live is amazing, mostly because it doesn't seem like it should work. I mean, over a hundred people, playing all sorts of instruments, coming in at different times and playing entirely different notes—and it all ends up sounding like one cohesive piece of music.

Fans of popular music typically find orchestral music intimidating. For the skittish, I recommend spending some time with Antonin Dvorak, or 'AnDvor,' as Buzzfeed might call him.

Dvorak wrote in almost every 'serious' form there was at the time, from chamber music to sprawling, cinematic symphonies.

He also spent a year in Iowa, which is about as mainstream and accessible a location as there is on Earth. Check out his *'American'* string quartet (the *"Quartet in F"*), which was written in the U.S., if you want an idea of what a Czech native thought this country sounded like.

"I should have called it 'Gun Violence and Obesity'."

The best thing about classical/serious/art/fancy music is that it's perfect for musical browsers like myself. If you had never heard a note of rock and roll, and were left to search through everything that is called 'rock and roll' without guidance, you would have to wade through an overwhelming amount of bad music.

With fancy music, the 'signal to noise' ratio is much different. You don't have to be knowledgeable about conductors, orchestras or chamber groups to surround yourself with first-rate music—just look for free music online and you'll encounter hundreds of great composers and remarkable compositions.

You can also build a respectable opera collection on the cheap. Opera may seem daunting, with its multiple languages and centuries-old storylines, but if you simply let the *sounds* get in your head, it will grab you.

In addition, with just a cursory understanding of a handful of plots, you can start to appreciate the heady mix of romance, intrigue and occasional murder that lies under the music. Once I was hooked, the binge listening began.

The CSO concert I attended also featured members of the Chicago Opera performing an excerpt from the opera *Nixon in China*.

That was impressive, but also challenging. *Nixon* is definitely not as hummable as any of the nineteenth-century Italian showcases. If you can imagine the History Channel producing a musical, you'll have some idea.

Any opera requires more suspension of disbelief than is required by musical theater. In a Broadway show, you have to accept that people suddenly break into song.

In opera, you have to accept that people wearing ridiculous costumes suddenly break into song, with perfect diction, while accompanied by fancy music.

Needless to say, I had no problem with any of that, and over the last several years, opera has become a significant part of my music library.

The weird thing is, while I've collected a lot of opera music, I still don't really know that much about opera. I don't know the names of many arias, I'm hazy about most of the plots, and I constantly confuse Verdi with Puccini.

For all I know, they were one enormously prolific person named Verdi Puccini. I'm not an opera aficionado, and yet I could listen to opera music for hours.

I was first exposed to opera through a play about the great diva, Maria Callas. I saw *Master Class,* which is about Callas' post-performance career as a teacher to private students.

The music intrigued me so much, I reverted to my high-school days and started checking out CDs from the nearest library. While retaining almost nothing I've learned as far as any *specific* opera is concerned, I fell in love with the *idea* of opera.

Whether it's melodramatic tenors, wailing sopranos, or chest-thumping baritones, opera delivers more drama and more mental illness than any other vocal art form. Sung by the right diva, madness can actually sound liberating.

The only opera I have seen on stage in its entirety was probably *Turandot,* but it might have been *Tosca.* There was either a shopgirl, or maybe it was a princess . . . and somebody was in love, and some character may have been stabbed, but I might be thinking of a different opera there.

My favorite part of whichever opera I saw was when one of the female characters was terribly upset about something and jumped from the top of a castle. Or it might have been a factory. The specifics don't matter. It *sounded* glorious.

Probably because of my background as a band geek, I've never found classical music, or even opera, too daunting. I have, however, been scared by jazz. I'm sure having Dizzy Gillespie stop his show to tell me to get back to my seat didn't help.

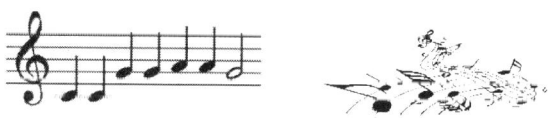

The image on the left represents 'normal' music. The other image is 'jazz.'

Maybe it's just flashbacks to my high school Dixieland jazz group, for which my band director had to write out each of my solos, since I didn't know how to create my own. Or maybe my OCD makes it hard for me to embrace improvisation, since I've always been a 'color *inside* the lines' sort of guy.

I won't attempt to define jazz. Other things I would have trouble defining include: right, wrong, God, love, and art. Jazz is the Zen of music genres. It is what it is, unless it isn't.

I've always thought that, on one level, jazz is a lot like baseball, or Buddhism. You have to be in the right head space to understand any of them. If you're not ready to embrace a different mindset, baseball is too slow, Buddhism is too esoteric, and jazz is too complicated.

You need some life experience to really 'get' jazz. I *heard* jazz at a young age, but I didn't know how to *listen* to it until I was older, and that was only because I stopped trying to figure it out.

The most appealing thing about jazz is how democratic it is. It is easily the most egalitarian form of music. In a jazz combo, there may be solo flights of improvisation that get the spotlight, but every instrument's voice is, well, instrumental.

Every kind of instrument is welcome at the party. There are jazz French horn players, jazz harmonica players, even jazz bassoonists. I've never heard of a jazz bagpiper, but I'm sure there is at least one. The only rule of jazz instrumentation seems to be that you get to play if you're willing to swing.

The 'swing' element is what's missing from what's frequently called 'smooth jazz.' Smooth jazz isn't real jazz any more than Velveeta is real cheese.

Smooth jazz is the musical equivalent of *The Big Bang Theory* (the TV show, not the cosmic event). It seems smart until you really listen to it, and then it just seems pointless.

Real jazz, whether it's a single tune, an album, or a concert experience, is always moving, and the best jazz is all about the *unexpected* destination, and that is what distinguishes it from other styles of music.

Even the most creative rock songs usually take the listener to one of a handful of familiar places.

It makes sense that jazz *goes* to many places, because it comes from all over the map. Basically, in the early twentieth century, spirituals, folk music, and the blues got together for a group hug, and jazz happened.

If I were asked to recommend a book to introduce someone to jazz, I would refuse. Instead, I would lock that person in a room, with a turntable, a pair of headphones, and the following vinyl albums:

Miles Davis, *A Kind of Blue*

John Coltrane, *A Love Supreme*

Ella Fitzgerald, *The Cole Porter Songbook*

Chet Baker, *Chet Baker Sings*

Django Reinhardt, *Djangology*

Charlie Parker, *Bird and Dizs*

Benny Goodman, *The 1938 Carnegie Hall Concert*

In the seventies, jazz took a sudden left turn and crashed into rock music. Here again, in 'jazz fusion,' Miles Davis would be at the top of any list. With *Bitches Brew*, Miles made jazz accessible to a generation raised on rock rhythms and sensibilities.

Beyond the groundbreaking and genre-busting musical elements, *Bitches Brew* is significant because it pissed off the purists, in the same way that Dylan did when he went electric at Newport. As far as I'm concerned, any music that rattles cages and annoys the 'in crowd' is worth exploring.

From the title to the cover art to the six individual tracks on the record, *Bitches Brew* scared the people who thought they were in charge of defining 'jazz' for the masses. Great music should, on occasion, frighten people.

Centuries ago, when music consisted of mostly droning, unison plainsong, somebody decided to add harmony, with different people singing different notes at the same time, and it scared people.

We don't tend to think of orchestral music as scary, but at the premier of Stravinsky's 'Rite of Spring,' audience members went from booing the unfamiliar sounds to fistfights to a riot *during the performance.*

Things were out of hand by intermission, the local police were called in, and the composer left the scene in fear before the performance was over. It wasn't exactly The Stones at Altamont (for one thing, the Hell's Angels weren't in charge of security), but for its time, it was a big deal.

Stravinsky scared the audience by breaking the unspoken rules. The arbiters of taste in Paris in 1913 had decided that ballet scores should be courtly and elegant. Stravinsky challenged that, and hundreds of well-dressed Parisians lost their minds.

Any artistic expression of something new is bound to scare somebody. Elvis Presley frightened people by bringing sex to popular music and appropriating rhythm and blues; The Stones scared people by bringing a dark side to rock and roll (and also appropriating rhythm and blues); Public Enemy and NWA scared people by speaking truth to power.

So, it's okay that *Giant Steps* by John Coltrane scares me. That way, I approach it with the respect it deserves. At my age, it's important for me, once in a while, to let some challenging music shake me out of my easy listening cocoon.

"You have to be able to play a long time
to play like yourself."

--Miles Davis

Old Hands

I was never a fan of Bob Seger. When I was younger, and he had radio hits, he always sounded like a tired old man reminiscing about being young and virile. Since I thought of *myself* as young and virile, and I knew *I* would never grow old, Bob Seger bored me.

Every other lyric of his seemed to be from the perspective of some guy who, when he was younger, had some moves and got some tail.

Also, he was strong, and he liked rock and roll. Now he's old, and he's not as strong, but he still likes rock and roll, I'm assuming as long as it's 'old-time.'

"Against the Wind" opens with 'It seems like yesterday . . . but it was long ago.' Yes, Bob, that's the way memory works. Even more simplistic are the lyrics to "Like a Rock":

Twenty years now, where'd they go?

Twenty years, I don't know.

I sit and I wonder sometimes where they've gone.

It's not surprising that there aren't many great lyrics in popular music about growing old. Rock and pop music is all about youth. Bands still tour when they're old, but they generally do songs that were written when they *weren't* old.

I don't begrudge bands like The Rolling Stones rocking into their seventies; I just think they should mix up their setlist with a few songs that address more mature concerns--making out a will, choosing an HMO, wearing reading glasses . . .

John Mayer wrote a pleasant enough song about aging called "Stop This Train." It has a beautiful guitar sound and a nice hook, but it's not very deep. He's *"scared of getting older"* because he's *"only good at being young."* Of course, he wrote it when he was twenty-nine, apparently unaware of how scary it can get.

At least The Beatles made being in your mid-sixties sound fun and perky, although now that I'm in my mid-fifties, that seems unlikely.

Bob Dylan wanted us all to stay *"forever young,"* but in "My Back Pages," he tells us he was *"so much older then,"* and that he's *"younger than that now,"* so I'm not sure what to glean from that.

Dylan's time-shifting aside, most of us are destined to do things in the other order, with the younger thing happening first.

For me, a Simon and Garfunkel song called "Old Friends" contains the most apt description of what 'old' feels like on the inside.

How terribly strange to be seventy

—Paul Simon

Strange is the absolute best word for how it feels to suddenly watch calendar pages spin by like in the background of a black and white movie. Stranger than *that* is the feeling you get when you finally admit to yourself that you *look* old.

Old man, look at my life. I'm a lot like you were

—Neil Young

I can't say time has treated me badly—if you never saw me walk, and were looking at me from a distance, you might even think I'm in my forties. Losing my hair never made me feel old—that started in my twenties.

A touch of gray kind of suits you anyway

—Robert Hunter

I have all my original teeth, even that one I thought I knocked out when I fell down face-first in my studio apartment in Chicago. It was a whole situation involving drinking, a mouse, and socks on a hardwood floor, but that's a story for another book.

You drag your feet to slow the circles down

—Joni Mitchell

By the way, other than Robert Hunter, all of the above songwriters were in their twenties when they wrote about what it's like to be old.

Although I was vaguely aware of getting older each year, the realization didn't have much significance for me. I didn't *feel* older with every birthday. I never thought of myself as old until one day, a few years ago, when I noticed something.

I was idly staring at my hands, you know, like people do. I may have been stoned. In any case, I suddenly realized that my hands had some explaining to do.

I was confused when my hands suddenly looked like the hands of an old man. You see, over the course of my life, the closest I've come to working with my hands was when I played the clarinet.

For some reason, though, my hands *look* like they've been hovering over an assembly line installing widgets for the last thirty years.

It was as if someone had Photoshopped Elmer's hands onto my obviously much younger body. Suddenly, I had Bob Seger's hands. Even my fingers seemed old.

In my head, I feel like I'm in my early forties, tops. In my southern hemisphere, on good days, I can convince myself I'm in my thirties. But no matter how ship-shape I may feel from top to bottom, these damned hands keep insisting that I'm getting old.

I worry about my hands, because stringing words together is the one talent I can still employ, and doing that is much easier when you can type.

As it is, there are times when one finger or another decides to stop sending sensations back to my brain, and once more than a couple of digits go numb, I end up correcting a lot of typos.

Of course, if my hands start to give up on me, I can always draw some comfort from the words of Yusuf Islam, who, as Cat Stevens, offered this helpful positive perspective--

If I ever lose my hands, I won't have to work no more.

--Cat Stevens

Truthfully, my worry has more to do with something I haven't done yet. For the last few decades, as to-do lists morphed into bucket lists, I have wanted to learn to play the piano.

Life kept getting in the way, I kept getting in my own way, and something was always a higher priority. Now, it may not happen *until* I'm sixty-four, but I haven't crossed "learn to play piano" off my list yet.

In popular music, I've always gravitated toward your piano-playing singer-songwriters. If Elton John's "Bennie and the Jets" comes on the jukebox, I'm the guy playing air piano. Air guitarists may get the chicks, but air pianists are real musicians.

I will definitely need some lessons to play an actual piano, but that hasn't stopped me from trying, every time I walk past one. For this reason, I avoid shopping malls at Christmas, and hotel lobbies. Security guards don't seem to appreciate my self-taught talent.

Over the years, I have learned the first part of the theme to *The Young and The Restless*. I do a passable version of the *Jaws* theme, at least the part with those two scary notes. I can also play a very slow version of "Close To You," right up to the part after the beginning.

As satisfying as that playlist might be, I want to learn how to play more, but every time I've tried to read piano music, I get frustrated. That's because, when you play piano seriously, apparently your left hand has to do something *entirely* different than your right hand.

This is conceptually *baffling* to me, as mystifying to me as drummers who sing. How is *that* possible? I'll cop to the fact eye hand coordination and fine motor skills were never my strong suits, even before my spinal cord started sending out random twitches.

But the idea of telling each of my hands to just do their own thing, playing different notes with different rhythms . . . well, it all just seems a tad improbable, don't you think? I have seen it done, though, so hopefully, my hands will keep working long enough for my brain to figure out how to do it.

Wow

It has been said that, in this era of streaming music and music subscriptions, the concept of *owning* music has become passé. If ownership means the ability to physically carry something with you, then I'll admit that's true, and I have mixed feelings about it.

It's true that I can't carry my music collection over to a friend's house, since most of my music is now stored in the Great and Mysterious Cloud, simply represented by a string of ones and zeroes.

I miss having a tactile connection to my music. Anytime I didn't have a musical destination in mind, it was very satisfying to flip through a foot locker filled with vinyl albums, pulling out just the right album.

Even with cassettes and CDs, browsing my collection was hands-on, and I felt more connected to the music if I was holding it in my hands. Not to mention the hours I spent reading 'liner notes'—I was able to learn everything from song lyrics to the names of the backup singers, and it all came *with* the music.

There is one advantage to stashing 'my' music in the ether. In the past, if I wanted to inflict my musical tastes on someone else, I was limited to what I could carry.

I would need to bring the actual albums to them, and ask if I could use their turntable. Or, if they were cassettes, I would have to bring one of those dorky cassette travel cases, and feel like Briefcase Boy all over again.

When I peruse my music library, I realize that I have a little bit of crazy that I have yet to mention--I'm a digital hoarder.

The only thing that distinguishes me from the guy sitting in a room filled with piles of old newspapers is that the things I acquire don't take up space. I have collected more music that I could possibly have time to hear.

I have huge collections of classical music that I own because they were $1.99 each. Was I familiar with, or intrigued by, specific composers, or definitive performances? Nope. It was a hundred and one pieces of music for two bucks.

In my music collection, there are songs I've never listened to. I'm not sure exactly *when* I will be in the mood to listen to a solo album by Agnetha Fältskog from ABBA. I don't know that there *is* a best time to kick back with the Bulgarian National Choir, but I have eight of their songs as well, just in case.

I am a card-carrying member of the last generation of humanity that will ever be amazed by new technology. Whenever some wireless cloud-based hyper-cyber thingie is announced, younger people either buy it or they don't, but they aren't, as a rule, 'wowed' by anything.

When I see a new device, able to do something I never knew I needed, my reaction is usually along the lines of "What strange sorcery is this?" When I unboxed my latest smartphone, I held it for moment like I was a prehistoric villager who had found Captain Kirk's tricorder.

On PBS I saw the violinist Joshua Bell play a duet with Sergei Rachmaninoff, over sixty years after Rachmaninoff died. A piano had been *programmed* to play the piano part exactly as it had been played by the Russian virtuoso decades before.

If this same performance had been observed a hundred years prior, people would have been fleeing the theater in terror, but this was PBS in 2009, so the audience simply applauded politely.

I believe, when you lose the capacity to say, "Wow," to things that never used to be *possible*, you stop fully experiencing the world.

Technology has given us access to an unprecedented *amount* of entertainment options although the percentage of *quality* entertainment has stayed fairly constant. But it's not just that the entertainment is out there—we expect it to be available to us the moment we hear about it. We're entitled to it.

I call this phenomenon 'entertainmentitlement,' and I've bought into the mindset myself. Recently, I heard that the Rolling Stones had played a gig in a small bar somewhere in Europe. That should have been all we needed to find the entire show in 4k HD video instantly, for free, shouldn't it?

When we couldn't, in fact, watch The Stones perform a special, unannounced show that took place thousands of miles away from the comfort of our home, we actually felt *irritated.*

We were almost angry at YouTube for denying us our inalienable right to watch what we want. We were worried that we had done something to offend the great God of Searches.

Never mind that, when I was younger, The Stones could have come through my *neighborhood* and if I didn't see them in person, I would have had to rely entirely on the description of friends who might have been there. "It was great, man. You should have seen it!"

So, I don't have access to every bit of music ever recorded. There are gaps in my library. Still, iTunes tells me that I have five thousand, one hundred and one songs. If I never acquired anything new, I would be able to play my music continuously for just over fifteen days without repeating a track.

My shrink would probably say I draw comfort knowing that the music is there, if I should happen to need it, and knowing that I will always be able to play the perfect piece for whatever mood strikes me.

He might also suggest that my music is taking the place of real personal relationships, that I am actually hiding in the songs to avoid dealing with the real world, and that I have to start paying for sessions or he will have to stop seeing me.

All of those things are true to some degree, but I'm not concerned. Once I understood that music was more effective than medicine or therapy in managing my particular brand of crazy, I found some peace.

It's very calming to embrace the belief that I'm never more than two or three songs away from regaining my grip.

As long as I have some device that, through some combination of clicks, taps, or button-pushes, lets me to hear my music, I don't worry about much of anything.

As long there is music within reach, I don't care if it's a transistor radio hidden under my pillow or a Bluetooth speaker streaming satellite radio.

We're constantly developing new ways of putting music in our ears, but we've lost something along the way. Most people today consume their music *a la carte*, collecting individual songs without any thought of how they might flow. Those people are philistines.

It used to be that vinyl albums, had at most, twelve or thirteen songs. Good musicians would spend a year or two communing with their muses, or doing drugs, then they would write some songs, choose the best dozen or so, and release those to the public.

For a good musician, twelve songs is enough to communicate a story, or take the listener down a new road. The great albums didn't need remixes or unreleased bonus tracks of dubious quality. Miles Davis only needed *five* pieces of music to create one of the greatest albums in jazz history.

I have five *thousand* songs to choose from that tell my story, but for your sake, rather than list them all, I've narrowed it down to twelve.

These are the recordings that I keep in my mental health first aid kit. Bear in mind, I am not licensed to *prescribe* any of this music to you. I just know what works for me.

Yo-Yo Ma
"Unaccompanied Suite No. 3 in C Major"

One man and one musical instrument, communicating volumes about the human experience. Bach wrote six of these, and for my Trinitarian friends, this one represents the Holy Ghost. I don't know about all that, but there is something supernatural going on here.

It's also a great ringtone. When people call me, I look incredibly cultured. Unfortunately, I don't always pick up in time, because I want to listen to the whole piece. At least my ringtone isn't 'Who Let the Dogs Out?"

Anne Sophie-Mutter
"Meditation" from Thaïs

In the Massenet opera 'Thaïs,' this melody is played between the scenes of the second act, but you don't need to understand Byzantine Egypt to appreciate it. The opera itself is a strange mix of religious fervor and erotic passion, which is how I would describe certain periods in *my* life.

New York Phil.--Thomas Schippers, conductor
"Adagio for Strings"

Sometimes the only way to get to a peaceful place is to strap yourself in and ride through the darkness. Samuel Barber's most well-known composition was used in the films *Platoon* and *The Elephant Man* to underscore tragedy, and it's been played at the funerals of FDR, JFK, and Princess Grace, but I've never thought of it as a downer.

Over the course of eight minutes, it goes to some sad places, but it's never maudlin. It swoops and swirls and builds and if you go *with* it, by the time you get to that F major chord at the end, you'll feel like your circuits have been rewired. In a good way.

Nat King Cole,
"Stardust"

I suppose this would also be considered a 'sad song,' since it's about lost love. But wrapped in this arrangement, with Nat Cole's voice navigating Hoagy Carmichael's serpentine melody, melancholy never sounded so life-affirming.

It's the sonic equivalent of sipping a perfect liqueur.

I watched a video of this on YouTube, and I rarely quote anonymous comments, but I think 'Anotheryou21' said it as well as I could have: *The secret was he sang the song from the inside out, and gave you time to get in there with him.*

John Coltrane and Johnny Hartman
"My One and Only Love"

Trane plays the Guy Wood melody all the way through, and you start to think, "There isn't much a singer could add here."

Then, at 2:18, Hartman comes in with the Robert Mellin lyrics, and everything, including love, starts to make sense.

If you smoke, you'll want a cigarette after hearing this. If you don't, you'll want to start.

Tommy James and the Shondells
"Crystal Blue Persuasion"

According to James, he wrote the lyrics based on words he saw in different parts of the Book of Revelation. Thankfully, the words he saw were 'crystal,' 'blue,' and 'persuasion,' and not the dark, violent, and freaky images found in the rest of the book.

Otherwise, he might have written a song called "Seven-Headed Beast." It's also possible the song is about amphetamines, but it hardly matters.

Whether it was inspired by the End Times or crystal meth, the song ended up being all about positivity, and it's like an audio s'more, with gooey layers of peace, love, and marshmallow.

Joni Mitchell
"Chelsea Morning"

I'm not a morning person. When I am forced to slip the bonds of slumber, I am never poetic. Usually, when I first get up, I'm barely verbal.

I'm sure all that would change if I woke up in the Chelsea Hotel, but until that happens, I can choose to see the morning through Joni Mitchell's eyes.

I *would* like to start my day with milk, toast and honey, and a bowl of oranges, too. And the line, "the sun poured in like butterscotch, and stuck to all my senses" is flawless metaphor. Add 'crystal beads' and 'incense owls' and it's like waking up in a Pete Max painting.

Miles Davis
"So What"

You might already know that this track is based on Dorian scales, and that the chords in the 'head' of the song comprise three perfect fourths followed by a major third. Good for you.

You don't, however, *need* to know those things to get inside this tune. Once you *are* inside, you don't need music theory at all, any more than you need a degree in architecture to appreciate the Empire State Building.

Prince and the Revolution
"Housequake"

Prince's music could be spiritual, profound, contemplative, visionary, and deeply personal. This is none of those things, but it is a veritable post-graduate treatise on the philosophy of funk. On a more personal note, the song's lyric mentions *Green Eggs and Ham*, which happens to be the first book I ever read.

Literary references aside, sometimes, the best way to get unstuck is to leave your mind out of the equation and reconnect with your body, no matter how broken down you might feel. I haven't danced in decades, but when this song kicks in, I feel like moving every part of me that still works.

Tower of Power
"What Is Hip?"

There are certain questions which have baffled the greatest minds in history. Is there a God? How did the Universe begin? Why does David Hasselhof have a career? Before we can answer those questions, we need to solve the underlying mystery of hipness.

In true Socratic fashion, songwriters Emilio Castillo and Doc Kupka never offer an easy answer, although they do suggest that *"sometimes, hipness is what it ain't."* However you *define* 'hip,' the horn section on this record is what you're describing.

Bob Dylan
"I Shall Be Released"

I've never seen the inside of a jail cell. The extent of my criminal activity has been smoking pot in places where that hasn't been *technically* legal at the time. The fact that I've never had to craft a shiv out of a toothbrush doesn't mean I've never felt like I was in prison.

Usually that prison was of my own construction, but it still felt like the walls were closing in. Whether you're incarcerated by your job, confined by a relationship, or just trapped in your head, four minutes with Dylan (and the otherworldly harmonies of the Band's Richard Manuel) will rehabilitate you.

The Tallis Scholars
"Miserere mei, Deus"

If I ever start to take music for granted, I listen to this. Gregorio Allegri's setting of the 51st Psalm caused quite a commotion in the early seventeenth century.

Not only was it forbidden by the Vatican to transcribe the music, you could only *perform* it at special services. That's not to mention the fact that you would be excommunicated, which was a *huge* deal. in seventeenth-century Rome.

There is a powerful, if apocryphal, story about "Miserere," which speaks to its transformative magic. The story says that a teenage Mozart heard the piece one morning, and was so consumed by it that he transcribed it from memory later that day, essentially creating the first 'bootleg.' I figure, if Mozart thought it was that important, I should give it a listen.

The words are, of course, in Latin, but you don't really need the words—you probably won't be singing along with this one.

All you need to know is that it's about asking for mercy, and that is something that has never gone out of style, musically speaking. Whether it's choristers in ornate cathedrals or blues singers in dive bars, everyone can use a little mercy.

In the big picture, 'wash me thoroughly from my wickedness' is not *that* far removed from "Take Me To The River."

I would offer that you can draw a line from Allegri's Baroque masterpiece imploring, *"Have mercy on me"* to Roy Orbison growling, *"Mercy!"* in "Pretty Woman," and extend that line all the way to Marvin Gaye's "Mercy, Mercy Me." It's not a straight line, but it is a line, nonetheless.

Conversations

By this point, you may have noticed that this book is as much about me as it is about music. You also may have realized that it's neither comprehensive nor authoritative.

What? No chapter about goth rock? No mention of EDM? Nothing about crunk?

Wait a minute--the author is just some guy we don't know, with a bunch of opinions—he's not an expert!

To which I say, true enough. So, to fill in some of the gaps, I reached out to some folks with first-hand music experience. I talked with people who have taught musicians their craft, people who have produced records, and people you might have heard on the radio.

I talked with one man who inhabits the music of Led Zeppelin, another who is responsible for making great pianists sound even greater, and *two* people who have devoted decades of their lives to an instrument that has worldwide popularity. I even found someone to definitively explain why songs get stuck in my head.

I also spent a little time with a man who isn't a singer or a songwriter, but whose life has intersected with Bob Dylan, B.B. King, and Bruce Springsteen. For that interview, I didn't do too much talking, but I was Really Listening.

According to a quote attributed to actor / comedian / painter / musician Martin Mull, "writing about music is like dancing about architecture."

I suppose that would make *interviewing* someone about music analogous to . . . finger painting about dancing about architecture, but analogies aren't really my forte.

The High School Band Director

Once I remembered how much marching band meant to me, I thought it might be fun to track down the man who was in charge, our band director, Mr. Giesler.

I was fairly certain that I wouldn't find him online, but I found someone from my graduating class who was friends with his daughter on Facebook.

She and I exchanged a couple of Facebook messages, set up a time to call him, and by the power of Zuckerberg, there I was, talking on the phone with my high school band director.

What do you say to someone with whom you haven't spoken in thirty-five years? After some small talk, *("How have you been since 1978?")*, I asked him how he came to be a high school band director.

As it turned out, though he started piano lessons in second grade, and played trumpet in high school and college band, his career started on a very different path.

I was a chemistry major, (but) after teaching chemistry ... I saw that my friends who were band directors were having a whole lot more fun than I was. So I went back to school.

I wondered what he thought was the key to making band fun for students, and he said,

The first thing you have to look at is the music itself, and the music has to be fun. You don't have to play the crap—the junk. We never did play 'boom boom dittum dattum wattum choo'.

I love that he caught himself swearing. And I'm grateful I didn't have to play any 'boom-boom-dittum-dattum-wattum-choo.'

His least favorite part of his job as band director?

Without a doubt it was all the politics. Let's put it this way: There wasn't a day went by that I wasn't putting out some kind of fire.

I must admit, I was totally unaware of any 'political' intrigue swirling around the campus at the time, but I recently learned about an admirable stand Mr. Giesler took when he became Quartz Hill High School's first music director. He refused to teach the band to play 'Dixie.'

You see, for reasons that were unclear to me in high school and make very little sense today, our school nickname was the 'Rebels.'

This, though we were located about a hundred miles from Los Angeles. It wasn't what you would call a place with tradition steeped in the Confederacy.

But there we were, the 'Mighty Marching Rebels.' Even at fourteen, I thought it was weird that our mascot was a military guy on a horse named 'Johnny Reb,' and that said mascot used to be called *Jubilation T. Cornpone.*

Also, until the mid-nineties (that would be the 1990s), the school emblem featured a Confederate flag.

Turns out, the 'Rebel' part was meant to be a tribute to the brave men and women who fought valiantly against . . . the local school district about where to put a new high school.

So it was just an unfortunate *coincidence* that *some* people were reminded of our nation's most tragic era when they saw a 'rebel' on horseback in a Confederate uniform with a Confederate flag!

In any case, I'll let Mr. G. take it from here:

> *It wasn't very long after we opened the school (in 1964) that the 'Dixie' stuff was going on—not in an ugly sort of way, just, maybe we could play it—the band boosters wanted to hear "Dixie."*

> *But I always managed to kind of wiggle around and wheel out of it, because I knew it would cause . . . consternation in some parts. And to this day, you do not hear the band play 'Dixie.'*

As I recall, we did play "The Star-Spangled Banner. It's militaristic, and it's based on a British drinking song, but at least it doesn't sound like it's celebrating antebellum life on a Mississippi plantation.

> *Early in my career, I took a job in a town called Basin, Wyoming. There were about twelve hundred people in the town, and about a hundred and twenty people in the high school. Out of that, we had maybe fifty or sixty that were in the band.*

> *We were going to play for the first football game, and first of all, I didn't have any brass players that weren't football players.*

> *So, (the rest of the band) is on the field, this little group of about twenty-eight or so. I raised my hands for the start of the 'Star-Spangled Banner,' and we only got a few measures, and we had to stop. So we started again.*

That happened three times before we were able to play all the way through. After that, whenever I started a band, first day of the year, the Star-Spangled Banner was always the first piece we learned.

I'm not sure what I expected when I started to talk to Mr. Giesler, but I know that if you wanted to film a public service announcement with a real teacher talking about why teaching matters, you couldn't do much better than this:

> *My main objective, through everything we did, was personal responsibility. It was never learning to play an instrument, learning to march . . . none of those things until they had personal responsibility.*

Twenty-eight years. That's how long his career was. Almost three decades of listening to out-of-tune trumpets, honking saxophones and squeaking clarinets.

Do the math—twenty-eight years multiplied by maybe six clarinets in each band, a hundred or so rehearsals each year, times at least five squeaks per rehearsal . .

That poor man had to endure *over nine thousand squeaks and squawks from clarinets alone!* I asked him how he survived all the wrong notes and out of tune horns. I assumed it was some combination of earplugs and medication, but Mr. Giesler simply said, *"Patience. And the desire to get out of the kids the very best they could do."*

Finally, I asked him a question that had been nagging at me for thirty-five years. Did *he* think we looked ridiculous in our gigantic uniforms? After a pause, he answered, *"Yes, in a way.*

I knew it! Incidentally, when his daughter Mary was setting this up, she asked me if I could give her some details about myself, to help her dad remember me. I told her I carried a briefcase, and apparently that's all he needed to hear. To some people, I'll always be Briefcase Boy.

The Mischievous Musicologist

Some novelty acts are so committed to the joke that the word 'novelty' seems unfairly disparaging. I first heard the music of P.D.Q. Bach on the *Dr. Demento Show*, and it wasn't long after that I was back at the library, trying to wrap my brain around this misunderstood composer.

The 'misunderstood' part comes from the fact that P.D.Q. Bach didn't actually exist. Yet despite the hardship of being *entirely fictional*, he was responsible for dozens of pieces of music, many of which are still performed today—

The Echo Sonata for Two Unfriendly Groups of Instruments

Grand Serenade for an Awful Lot of Winds and Percussion

The Stoned Guest, a 'half-act opera'

P.D.Q. Bach was created by composer and musicologist Peter Schickele, though Schickele would say 'discovered.' Take eighteenth century classical music, throw in a bunch of wacky sound effects, and add a layer of musical inside jokes, and you have the music of P.D.Q. Bach.

He has won *four* Grammy awards for his 'discovery.' That's more than Elvis Presley, Chuck Berry, Jimi Hendrix, and Led Zeppelin *combined*. That says more about the Grammys than it does about P.D.Q. Bach.

And sure, those Grammys were for Best Comedy Recording, but fourteen albums (spanning four decades), three 'best of' compilations, two DVDs and an audiobook serve as a testament to the importance of P.D.Q. Bach. Who, as I may have mentioned, did not actually exist.

Beyond the funny stuff, Peter Schickele is also a well-respected composer of chamber music, with concerts of his more 'serious' works performed by some of the country's most esteemed string quartets. If that's not enough variety for you, he also wrote the soundtrack for the classic seventies eco/sci-fi film, *Silent Running*.

I spoke with Peter Schickele by phone to make sense of how all this fits together. Early in our conversation, I told Schickele I listened to his albums in high school, and although I thought they were funny, I wasn't always sure why—I didn't exactly get all the jokes. I wondered if he ever had audiences or reviewers who didn't 'get it' . . .

> *I don't know about not <u>getting</u> the joke—I certainly have had audiences and reviewers who don't like what's going on. There are some classical music fans who feel that classical music is sort of a sacred thing and should not be satirized.*

> *Professional musicians tend to be fans, and I think it's because they recognize that I'm not putting down classical music; I'm just having fun with it.*

> *I've always worked on a lot of different levels, not out of a calculated attempt to appeal to everybody, but because I worked with what I think is funny.*

I think a lot of things are funny, from very sophisticated musical jokes to complete slapstick, so it's all in there.

There are a lot of levels to laugh at, and if some of the things go by some of the people in the audience, that's fine with me.

I had read he was an accomplished bassoonist, but he told me the bassoon wasn't his first instrument—

I was not a child prodigy in music at all. I played clarinet first. My mother had played in college, and she still had her old clarinet, so I started playing that.

There was a good clarinetist in the Fargo area, where we lived at the time, and I went to take lessons from him.

He listened to me, and after about a minute he said, 'You've got so many bad habits on the clarinet that it would be easier for you to start another instrument.

Really, the bassoon isn't usually *any* kid's first instrument, since it's over four feet long, and it's impossible to look cool playing one.

Also, a decent one costs about $10,000. I guess if you're a kid playing the bassoon in Fargo, North Dakota, you're destined for a career in comedy . . .

I was a big Spike Jones fan when I was ten years old. He had a very funny stage show, and that was the bond.

I had a theater in the basement of my house, and my brother and I would write plays, and put them on with my friends. So it was this theatrical side that appealed to me.

I put together a little band in imitation of Spike Jones, called Jerky Jems and His Balmy Brothers. Consisted of two clarinets, violin and tom-tom.

I wrote arrangements of things like the "Song of the Volga Boatmen," attempting to be funny. I'm glad there was no videotape in those days.

Making funny music with clarinets, violins, and even tom-toms is one thing, but P.D.Q. Bach's music is also known for its use of less 'traditional' instruments:

- the *'left-handed sewer flute'*
- the *'dill piccolo'*
- the *'pastaphone'* (made from uncooked manicotti)
- and the *'lasso d'amore'* (also known as a *'bloogle'* or a *'corrugaphone'*—essentially, an empty tube that you swing in a circle to 'play').

There's also one where you hold a clear plastic tube in a u-shape—you blow into it like a flute—and you hold the other end in your hand, and there's wine in it—it's actually a very difficult instrument to play.

Perhaps his most famous invention is the 'tromboon,' a trombone/bassoon hybrid which came about in one of those flashes of inspiration that distinguish true genius.

> *I invented that when I was in junior high school—I took my bassoon reed . . . and put it into a trombone.*

It makes sense that young Peter Schickele would end up with at least one foot in the world of comedy, but why the connection to Bach?

He acknowledged that the world of P.D.Q. Bach might be a hard sell today, since not many people are looking for music from the Baroque Era, let alone *parodies* of Baroque music.

Ironically, new technology helped jump-start P.D.Q.'s career. When this elaborate gag started, in the sixties, the newfangled 'long-playing' album had become popular, and for the first time, LPs allowed the release of 'complete sets' of music by composers, and according to Schickele,

> *There was a 'baroque backlash'—people were tired of 'yet another' Vivaldi concerto.*

Peter Schickele's split musical personality was in full bloom by the mid-sixties. In addition to now-annual concerts of P.D.Q. Bach 'music,' he was also arranging records by folk icon Joan Baez.

I asked him about the overlap between folk music and classical music, two worlds whose only common ground might be the insufferable purists who are in each camp . . .

> *By the time I was working with Joan Baez, the 'purist' time had already gone* (once Dylan 'plugged in' at Newport).

> *But there was a trend of using classically trained composers* (to arrange folk records) *and it was a positive experience—it wasn't a case of doing something I didn't enjoy just to put food on the table.*

Among those records, incidentally, is one of the purest and least cheesy holiday discs ever recorded. Simply called *Noel*, it's Christmas songs you've heard a million times, but for once, they're not buried under layers of studio tricks, 'modern' arrangements, and schmaltz.

> *That's one of the few albums of mine that I listen to myself. I was very fortunate with Joan, in that she never told me how to make an arrangement.*

> *We just decided what key, and how many verses, and whether she was gonna play guitar.*

Unfortunately, when he was arranging for Baez, he never let his musical *comedy* instincts take over—it would have been great to hear this angelic soprano voice doing "Good King Wenceslas" with a tromboon solo thrown into the mix, but he laughed and said it wasn't a problem.

Nope . . . I seem to have a pretty well-ordered mind for that sort of thing. I can work on a serious piece and a P.D.Q. Bach piece at the same time.

Sometimes, I'm not sure whether they're gonna end up being one or the other.

I wondered whether he ever felt trapped in his alter ego. Did audiences at his serious concerts expect there to be jokes? Is that frustrating?

It is, sometimes. But I've just been calm about it. I've gotten a lot of commissions, and I've had a lot of my (serious) music recorded, particularly chamber music.

There's a string quartet in L.A. (The Armadillo String Quartet) which does my serious chamber music, and we just did our twenty-third annual concert.

Despite his unconventional sense of humor (an early P.D.Q. album features a version of Beethoven's *Symphony No. 5* with sports announcers providing the 'play-by-play'), his path never intersected with the more psychedelic elements of the sixties:

I was never a tripper myself, and I never got involved with the real psychedelic stuff. I was a big fan of the popular music of the sixties, though. I think it was an amazing time.

(For example) there was a group that had a hit with a rock version of "Ding Dong, The Witch Is Dead," and the instrumental interlude was a literal quote of a seventeenth-century dance by Michael Pretorius.

For the trivia buff, the band was called The Fifth Estate, and they hit #11 on the charts in 1967. I was surprised at how aware of psychedelic rock Schickele. He liked Zappa, who frequently blurred the line between novelty and experimental music.

In fact, minimalist pioneer Phillip Glass, a classmate of Schickele, helped build one of his most famous sound contraptions—the Hardart.

Named for a chain of 'automats' that were popular during the Great Depression, it's featured in P.D.Q. Bach's "Concerto for Horn and Hardart."

In performance, a musician would need to put coins in the machine's slot to get at the instruments they needed to play.

Schickele also created two children (neither of whom are fictional), and they're both in indie-rock bands. Would P.D.Q. Bach have been into the indie-rock scene? *"He certainly would have felt an empathy with indie people!"*

After taking a minute to remind myself that we were talking about a fictional composer, he did some free association on a few real European composers. It was like a handy study guide from a very cool professor.

Shostakovich*: "One of the things I like about Shostakovich is that he would make very serious music, and almost funny, certainly circus-like music in the same symphony."*

Debussy*: "An extremely important composer in the direction that early twentieth century music took, but not very close to me in personality."*

Tchaikovsky: *"There's a lot of vintage Russian bombast* (great band name—Vintage Russian Bombast). *My favorite Tchaikovsky may be the ballet scores. I love the short pieces where the dancers 'show off,' where it's not part of the story."*

Wagner: *"He's not a composer I warm to, but he was absolutely amazing in his importance in the development of music, in terms of orchestration.*

My basic problem with Wagner is that concept of endless melody. It's not something that I think is necessarily a good idea. I like operas where you have this number, then that number, then the next number."

Whereas *my* basic problem with Wagner would be his blind, raging anti-Semitism, but I suppose endless melody is tedious, as well.

Who does he consider most similar to himself, in terms of personality?

Probably Mozart. I'm a big fan of the Mozart divertimenti and the early symphonies that have a quality that's not funny, but sorta witty. He has the combination of the sublime and the humorous that makes for great music.

Stravinsky is another big influence on me. He's another composer who has humor in his music without it necessarily being billed as humorous.

When I asked which composers could have used *more* of a sense of humor, he simply said, without hesitation, *"Elgar."* That would be Sir Edward Elgar, composer of such toe-tappers as "Pomp and Circumstance" and "The Saga of King Olaf."

Edward Elgar (1857-1934), enjoying a joke.

Peter Schickele may have one foot firmly planted in the eighteenth century, but his career moves forward. There probably won't be a world tour for P.D.Q. Bach, for a very valid reason.

There's a lot of talking in a P.D.Q. concert, and more importantly, *"I'm addicted to puns, and puns are the hardest things to translate."*

Shickele assured me there will be more to the P.D.Q. story, because *"I keep discovering more and more music by him."* But getting back to the present day, Schickele was excited about a new work he'll be premiering soon. . . .

It's a serious piece, but the last movement is variations on a pirate tune. It's an original tune, but it <u>sounds</u> like a cliché pirate song.

I'm very pleased, because I'm gonna invent a new musical direction. When it really gets swaggering at the end it's gonna be played 'AARGHissimo'!

The Harp Diva

Some of the most interesting music ever recorded is music that not only challenges boundaries, but erases them entirely. For that reason, I wanted to reach out to Jill Flomenhoft.

I met Jill in my other incarnation, as a food writer. Before I knew about Jill's musical genre-bending, I knew her as a purveyor of gourmet mashed potatoes. Her L.A. shop did nifty things like *black truffle* infused mashed potatoes.

That would be gift enough to the world, but she has the music thing going on, too. Jill plays the harp, and in addition to the conventional harp repertoire, she has played in the poetry scene, and her harpitude has been featured on records by artists ranging from Postmodern Jukebox to Compton-based rapper Glasses Malone.

Before I talked with Jill, the only person associated with the harp whom I could name was Harpo Marx. Harpo once described himself as "the most famous harp-playing, non-speaking comedian in history."

He was self-taught, and never read music, though he composed several pieces that are in the standard harp repertoire.

Jill told me that Harpo was unusual in another way, in that he used all ten of his digits, whereas most players don't use their pinkie fingers.

Other than what I saw in Marx Brothers movies, my harp literacy was limited to the logo on the Guinness bottle, so it seemed logical to ask Jill about drinking. Specifically, I wondered whether the harp scene was as party-oriented as other music scenes.

> *I certainly enjoy a recreational beverage. However, when I am performing, I cannot have any alcohol because it affects my motor skills.*

> *I don't know how my fellow musicians, like guitarists-- how these people go out on stage just completely wasted and have the greatest night . . .*

I suggested that the key might be the number of strings involved. It's probably easier to drunkenly strum *six* strings than *forty-seven*.

I suggested that Guinness could be a potential tour sponsor for her, and she said, *"I would love it, but I think they would be more inclined to sponsor a harper than a harpist..."*

The pretend journalist in me was hoping I had stumbled upon a controversy that was ripping apart the harp community, but in fact, it's just a semantic distinction.

As a rule, if it sounds like Appalachia, then the person playing is a 'harper.' If it sounds like an eighteenth century wedding, the musician is called a 'harpist.'

My mind went to other, less obvious derivations—if someone is a harp virtuoso, are they 'harptastic'? I call Jill Flomenhoft the 'Harp Diva' because that's what she calls herself. But as to whether she has ever exhibited any diva behavior,

You know, honestly, I think the harp is more of a diva than I am. It's a very finicky instrument with a lot of . . . specific environmental requirements.

I arrive early, and set it up onstage. When I get there, I need to spend twenty to thirty minutes manually tuning each string, because temperature and humidity affect what's going on with the instrument, just like with the human body.

I figured she must need to keep her home as climate-controlled as a spaceship to keep her harp in tune between gigs, but she said,

You're pretty much going to be tuning every day. There's not much you can do. In fact, if it's already onstage, and there are several performers before me, the harp can go out of tune before I start playing.

If you haven't spent much time on harp-related websites, don't worry. I have you covered. Harp.com, the Harp Society, Harp to Harp . . . I also checked out the site for Lyon & Healy, who have been building harps in Chicago since Lincoln's administration.

There's no other way to spin this –harps aren't cheap. If you're harp shopping this holiday season, the least expensive model on the L&H site goes for $11,500.

They occasionally award prizes to talented harpists, but the prize is typically *two thousand* dollars, which might buy you a couple sets of strings.

I found four used harps for sale on Craigslist, including a steal on a cherry wood Venus Prodigy model for seventy-five hundred bucks.

I didn't want to dwell on the cost issue, but Jill acknowledged it matter-of-factly, and with a laugh added, *"That's why I like playing next to one, because it looks like I'm expensive."*

As down to earth and casual as I found Jill to be, she told me that she occasionally dons the flowing gown most people have in mind when they picture a harpist, and she had an understandable reason:

> *The long flowing gown is because you're sitting on your bench, and the harp is positioned between your knees.*

Jill's harp was made in 1989 by an Italian company named Salvi. It has a mahogany finish, and is considered three-quarter size, with only forty strings instead of the forty-seven on a concert grand.

Again, practicality played a part—*"I love it because I can transport it in the Prius."* There's a new ad campaign for Toyota—"Get a Prius, and you can take your harp *with* you!"

Does she ever embellish her harp with a little bling?

> *Yes, and I'm interested in blinging her out more. If I'm doing a wedding, or a garden party, I'll wrap a garland around it, giving it that 'Midsummer Night's Dream' feeling.*

> *I did a party for the 'end of the world' on the Mayan calendar and I used feathers, and fur . . . sort of a Burning Man, tribal style.*

Musically, I was curious as to whether she was limited to the natural sounds of the harp strings, or if she has used effects, like a guitar player would with 'wah-wah' pedals and other doodads, to use the technical term.

> *I am in the middle of exploring this. I do have a little pickup that was added 'aftermarket' so I have the ability to plug in through a quarter-inch cable that then picks up the sound off the soundboard. I'm experimenting with using effects pedals right now.*

Since my reference points are more rock than harp, I had to know if there were ever a gig in which she was so in the moment that she considered taking a page from Pete Townshend's book and smashing her harp at the end of a performance.

> *That would be a sight. That would be amazing, but you'd have to be really careful. The harp has tons of pressure on the soundboard, and harps that are not well-conditioned have been known to explode, so it might actually be really dangerous.*

That's what we're looking for—some danger with our harp music! In point of fact, harp players were frequently in danger during the reign of Elizabeth I. It seems Liz thought they were stirring up discontent, with all their seditious madrigals and treasonous, gentle folk music.

Given that I knew how gangsta the harp scene could be, I brought up another potentially divisive subject: the ages-old debate between pedal harps and lever harps! If you're not up on your harp classification, in simple terms, pedal harps allow you to change keys more easily.

Jill began to explain that the pedals are attached to rods that are inside the long slender column, and the rods connect to mechanisms at the top of the harp, and I moved on quickly, because I was afraid she would spoil the magic. It was like seeing the projectors in Disneyland's Haunted Mansion—it ruined the ride for me.

At any rate, I just wanted to know if there were ever a feud between pedal purists and lever loyalists, analogous to the East Coast/West Coast rap turf war in the nineties.

> *I'm pleased to report that those of us who play the harp are evolved. The east coast harpists I've met are wonderful and we have a mutual admiration society.*

> *But pedal versus lever, that's a whole other conversation, and it can push some buttons.*

As to whether there are any personality traits that might make someone a good harpist, she said, *"My goodness . . . I think they've gotta be a bit eccentric, right? I mean you're taking on this thing . . . I guess it might be a bit showy."*

How does one end up playing the harp? I don't recall that being one of the choices when we were asked to pick an instrument for marching band.

What compels someone to take up playing an instrument that costs more than some cars, requires constant maintenance, and barely fits in a Prius? Why not a fifty-dollar acoustic guitar? Why the harp?

> *As a little kid, I had some piano, but only for maybe one or two years. The rest of my childhood was spent as an avid music junkie, an obsessive fan and listener. Then, I decided to get into the harp in college.*
>
> *It was really a case of 'ignorance is bliss.' It's so cumbersome, it becomes an entire lifestyle choice. You really don't know exactly what you're getting into, especially since I decided at the age of seventeen. I joke that the instrument must choose you.*
>
> *My mom would bring us to see* The Nutcracker *and there are such beautiful harp cadenzas in Tchaikovsky.*
>
> *Also, there was a lot of harp featured in Carmine Coppola's score to* The Black Stallion, *which was really big when I was growing up.*
>
> *And of course there's that wonderful piece on Stevie Wonder's* Songs in the Key of Life, *"If It's Magic," which features the jazz harpist Dorothy Ashby. I just thought, why do we not have more access to this instrument?*

Even if, on some level, you get why someone might want to play the harp, how does that world come to intersect with hip-hop?

Jill beat me to the punch by suggesting 'Harpists With Attitude' (whose albums would naturally banned for their explicit content). She then shared the story of how she found her way from the recital hall to the hip-hop studio:

> *I moved to L.A. and learned to play the instrument in the early nineties, and this was the golden age of hip-hop.*
>
> *This was an amazing time, when you look at A Tribe Called Quest, Souls of Mischief, and Dr. Dre discovering Snoop Dogg, and a lot of amazing emcees.*
>
> *It really felt like the music fit as a soundtrack for your life in L.A.—as you were rolling down Sepulveda, this was the music that was on the radio.*
>
> *It felt like the perfect time and place. I couldn't help but be influenced by that music, and really pay attention.*

As much as I understood the influence, I couldn't get past the disconnect in my mind between the gritty realities of hip-hop and the posh world of the harp. After all, the U.K. still employs someone with the title, "Official Harpist to the Prince of Wales."

I find that contrast compelling, putting those worlds on a crash collision course. What's neat is that so much hip hop, with sampling techniques . . .

Let's say they want a little treble theme that ends up being a repeating figure through the entire track—these translate really well onto the harp.

When I suggested she might be trying to 'dirty up' the harp just a bit, she was quick to answer, *"Absolutely."* Incidentally, I called Jill out for using the word, 'neat' in the context of hip-hop, and she said, *"What should I have said? Fresh?"*

Then I realized I didn't know, either. Besides, if you're 'rolling down Sepulveda' with a *harp*, 'neat' makes sense.My guess would be that audiences at hip-hop shows aren't exactly expecting to see a harp, with or without bling . . .

I get comments all the time from audience members who've never actually seen a harp in person, and I always invite them up to strum a little.

I want the harp to be accessible to the community. I don't want it to be up in the ivory tower. We can't let this gorgeous tradition fade. Some of these 'analog' traditions are really beautiful.

I hear from people all the time who say, 'I've always wanted to play the harp.' It's as relevant today as it ever was, but we still think of it as belonging in an eighteenth century parlor.

I've never really cared whether a style of music is 'relevant.' After all, I listen to Andy Williams. In the hands of Jill Flomenhoft, the harp definitely has relevance; she's dragging it, plucking and screaming, into the twenty-first century.

The Tribute Act

There are only a few acts that take 'tribute' to an entirely new place, precisely recreating vintage performances in details ranging from the lighting plot to the color of the lead singer's scarves. One of the most popular of these is the Chicago-based band, Led Zeppelin 2—The Concert Experience.

I spoke with the group's 'John Paul Jones' about the challenges of playing an iconic rock figure. A versatile and talented multi-instrumentalist in his own right, Matthew Longbons trained as a jazz trumpeter, but he didn't grow up in a musical bubble--

I discovered an acoustic guitar when I was thirteen or fourteen. It was the early nineties, so I was definitely one of the kids wearing a flannel shirt and a pair of Chuck Taylors, but I did learn how to play "Stairway to Heaven."

He has also been an in-demand session bass player for everything from TV commercials to online ads, and he's logged a lot of studio time.

He toured with cult favorites The Ghettobillies in the 2000s, but "*there comes a point when you live in a van for 250 nights a year when it starts to get old--after a decade.*"

It stands to reason that, for creative musicians, playing a tribute gig in which you more or less have to stick to the script, would be tedious, or at the least unsatisfying. The musical equivalent of a call-center job.

I have a friend who played with a female-fronted Devo cover band in New York (DEVA), and he said he didn't feel that way at all, since "*the script is so great.*" Matthew would agree, and added:

> *I still get a challenge out of the fact that I have to play piano and mandolin and bass, so I'm doing a ton of different things. I won't say how underrated John Paul Jones is, but maybe I hadn't noticed . . .*

I assumed they played songs *other* than "Stairway to Heaven," but with nine studio albums containing eighty-one tracks, and countless setlists, how do they choose which Zeppelin era to recreate?

> *We've done several, and at this point we've done almost all of it once. If we go into a new market, or at a festival, where all the people might not be there to hear the band, we do kind of a middle of the road, 'hits' type show.*

When we do Chicago, we do multiple nights, and we might do theme shows. We've planned a whole tour around the 'Physical Graffiti' album, with multimedia clips from that era that augment the show. We've also done their live albums.

My favorite part of Zeppelin's live discography is during "Stairway," when Robert Plant asks the crowd, "Does anybody remember laughter?" It was an ad lib that Plant wanted edited out, but thankfully, Jimmy Page insisted on keeping it in.

People who go to *Led Zeppelin 2: The Concert Experience* expect to hear that line, along with Plant's weirdly non-descript description of "Stairway," which he intros by saying *"I think this is a song of hope."* There are rules to this sort of thing:

There are two songs we have to play every night— "Stairway to Heaven" and "Dazed and Confused" because we're sticking true to their sets, and that's what they did.

The only time we got away without doing those was in one of our specialty shows. We did a set called '1970,' where we only did the first three albums.

The next night, we did '1980,' so we essentially did six hours of music over two nights without repeating a single song.

Although he plays "Dazed" and "Stairway" *every* night, Matthew doesn't hate either one—he reserves that hatred for a different Zeppelin classic—

The song "Rock and Roll."' I hate it, because it's covered poorly by everybody, sometimes including us. It's hard to play well, and everybody knows it.

Sadly, no matter which songs they're doing, it seems Robert Plant has very little interest in hearing his doppelganger . . .

Through mutual friends, before Robert Plant split up with Patty Griffin, when he lived in Austin . . . he knew who we were, because we had some mutual friends

We played at a pretty respected venue there called Emo's, and we extended an open invitation to him, but it never came to fruition.

It's one thing to sing and play like Zeppelin, and even to give the fans the 'expected' ad libs, but rock bands have larger-than-life personalities. Are any of them similar to their counterparts *offstage*? Is their 'Robert Plant' as flamboyant as the real deal?

Onstage, he definitely has the capability to command and capture an audience. He's a very well-respected frontman in the metal community, but he's also a bartender and a bar manager, so he has an extremely practical side when he needs to.

For the rest, it's hard to say . . . our guitarist is probably the closest. Our drummer has a lot of the traits of John Bonham, but he doesn't drink, which is kind of the fundamental opposite.

Original bands sometimes have rivalries with other bands, so it seemed logical that LZ2:TLE might see another tribute band as a 'competitor' for the same audience--

Not really. We just choose to ignore the fact that any other ones exist. I mean, if people are working, that's great.

The only time we hear about it is when the crews and bouncers that we've worked with in some places say that some of the other ones are a bit trickier to deal with.

We're all pros that have been doing this for a long time. We know how to do a sound check, and be nice to everybody. We have no delusions of grandeur that we're anything but what we are.

Having worked the other side of concerts, I get that you should have an act when you're on stage, but you don't need to have it from the minute you walk in the door."

The lesson: *nobody* appreciates a 'method-acting' Robert Plant.

The guys in LZ2:TLE may not be channeling the Actor's Studio, but unlike many tribute bands, they see themselves as actors and not just singers:

It's the crux of how we think of ourselves. It's like a musical. We're always trying to take costuming, and makeup and other elements to a higher level.

The great thing about being in Chicago is, if you know a couple of theater designers, you can just show them a picture and get very close.

We definitely look at it as theater. We're making an investment to set ourselves apart, as a touring theater thing, rather than a cover/tribute band. (That's why) our show is called The Live Experience.

We play with four people, in the same format they did live. Other bands use six or seven people, including John Bonham's son, that work on recreating it note-perfect, but they're out there with three guitar players, a separate piano player, a separate bass player . . .

With us, if it's not something that can be pulled off with myself, a guitar player, a drummer and a singer, we don't do it. And we choose from all of the live versions and sometimes bootlegs, so we don't play note perfect.

I figured his demographic would be primarily sixty-year old men, and they are there, but surprisingly, another group loves the 'Experience.'

> *There's people who were teenagers in the seventies, but at our 'all ages' shows, the first two rows are thirteen to eighteen year old kids. I think it's a sign of good parenting.*

I've always held the notion that playing in a tribute band is, in one sense, more difficult than playing in a successful original band. The key difference is the expectation.

If I had seen the 'real' Led Zeppelin in concert in 1974, I would have expected to hear some songs I knew, but I wouldn't have had any expectation of how they would be played.

Fans at a tribute show expect to hear the songs, *and* they expect to hear them performed *exactly* the way they were played in their first incarnation. They are coming to worship the band, and any deviation from the liturgy is blasphemy.

> *It's true, and I feel it's warranted. The original band was responsible for two very different things—the creation of the music, and the execution.*
>
> *But if somebody's doing a tribute thing, you are entirely on the execution / re-creation side. You had nothing to do with the creation of it, so you damned well better execute it right.*

I love hearing the music of an original band playing music and singing words that came from their hearts, and if a band is still together touring, I would rather see the original band.

But--if it's not possible to see that band in its original incarnation, because the members don't get along, or they're too old, or too dead . . . and some talented musicians are willing to duplicate the experience for me, I would pay for that.

It is not an easy gig, because if your 'tribute' is just playing and singing in costume, it can end up just being creepy, like the robot Lincoln in Disney's Hall of Presidents.

Since the fans are there to see their idols, a good tribute band needs to do more than *sound* like the band; they need to inhabit the original group's world. The illusion is easier to sustain if the guys paying 'tribute' to a classic band genuinely respect that band.

> *I put people like Plant and Page on the same level with Bach and Mozart—I'm not trying to elevate all rock stars to that classical level, but I believe, in two hundred years, that's the music people will be listening to.*

> *We're no more of a 'cover band' than the Chicago Symphony Orchestra, it's just a smaller production.*

The best tribute bands re-animate the source material, in the same way that an orchestra re-animates Beethoven or Tchaikovsky. It also helps to have Led Zeppelin songs as your 'script.' It's probably much harder to make a living in a Strawberry Alarm Clock tribute band.

The Accordion Authorities

I don't play the accordion. I've never thought, "How cool would it be to play the accordion?" For that matter, I'm not entirely sure I could *hold* an accordion. Despite these seeming obstacles to accordion fandom, I have become surprisingly informed on the subject.

It started the way most online searches go. Looking up things on the web isn't always productive for me, because I get distracted as easily as a Dalmatian at a dog park for the first time.

I start looking up information related to one specific thing, and an hour later I'm wandering aimlessly through cyberspace.

You've experienced this. You're trying to find an episode of *Punky Brewster*, but then you see a video of Paget Brewster, where she's reading James Joyce, so then you start searching for Joyce, except instead you end up watching videos of that lunatic evangelist, Joyce Meyer.

In this case, one minute I'm researching Grammy trivia, then I find out about the whole polka category kerfuffle, and the next thing I know, I'm interviewing accordion experts.

Before interviewing anyone, I needed to arm myself with some relevant facts. I wasn't raised in an accordion-friendly home (beyond watching Myron Floren with my parents on the *Lawrence Welk Show*), but I had a feeling there was more to the accordion than wheezy renditions of "Lady of Spain."

Here we see an accordionist playing the traditional lament, "I Wish I'd Learned A Smaller Instrument

I was surprised to learn that even musicians who play the accordion are ambivalent about it. Tom Waits is credited with saying, *"A gentleman is someone who can play the accordion, but doesn't."* Undeterred, I dove into the rabbit hole, absorbing random facts along the way.

I learned that the accordion as we know it was created in the early nineteenth century, and that Tchaikovsky included parts for it in his "Orchestral Suite No. 2 in C major," and that Brian Jones played one on some Rolling Stones records.

I learned that there are chromatic and diatonic versions of the instrument, but that sort of technical distinction didn't explain the soul of the accordion, or its worldwide reach.

It goes without saying that Scandinavians love accordions. There are several 'folk-metal' bands in Finland who feature the accordion, as you might expect. The most notable of these is Turisas whom you probably know from their headlining set at Paganfest.

I discovered that accordion music is popular in places as diverse and far-flung as Brazil, Colombia, Bosnia, and Herzegovina.

Here in the U.S., the 'piano accordion' has been the official musical instrument of San Francisco since 1990, approved by the city council in a 6 to 4 vote. I am curious to know the reasoning behind the 'nay' votes.

While this was all fascinating, I needed to talk to someone who had more hands-on experience with my newfound favorite instrument, someone who is in the bellows of the beast, as it were. Then I learned about a magical place near the shores of Lake Superior.

If you only visit one accordion museum this year, make it the World of Accordions Museum in Superior, Wisconsin. I did a little detective work (actually, I just called the museum) and had the chance to speak with the lovely woman in charge of the museum, Helmi Strahl Harrington.

I was worried early on in our chat, when Helmi told me she didn't want me to write anything "pejorative" about accordions, or the people who play them.

Being a comedian, I was conflicted, since mocking is a big part of what I do. But by the time we finished talking, I was ready to get out of the satire business and sign up for accordion lessons.

The museum houses more instruments than all other accordion museums combined. Yes, there are others, the most famous of those being the Alfred Mirek Russian Accordion Museum in Moscow. This proves that, in the tense Cold War between Russian and American accordionists, we won.

Helmi Harrington explained why it makes sense . . .

> *It's appropriate that America, the melting pot of the world, has the finest accordion collection. Many would have been brought over from other countries by immigrants who cherished their homeland traditions through the music expressed (by) accordions, from one generation to another.*

About two thousand tourists visit every year, in addition to specialty scholars and researchers from all over the world who come to experiment with instruments. When I asked her if she had fielded any unusual requests, she said,

> *Oh yeah, all the time. At least twice a year, we get somebody who calls in who wants a nude accordion player.*

In the past, if I thought of accordions at all, I would have thought 'wholesome,' and not 'saucy.' As it happens, though, Helmi gets a kick out of subverting the stereotypes:

> *One of the things I like best is showing tourists our collection of naked ladies."*

To clarify, those would be *accordions* with *pictures* of naked ladies. To my knowledge, the museum does not have a room filled with *actual* naked ladies.

World of Accordions showcases rare customized models, some of which fold up in unusual ways, and some of which look like guitars. I'm not sure if there's one that folds up, *and* looks like a guitar *with* a naked lady on it, but if there is, it would be at World of Accordions.

A top-quality, custom-designed accordion can cost as much as fifty to sixty-five thousand dollars. When I asked what went into a sixty-five thousand dollar accordion, she answered, "*Guess what it <u>wouldn't</u> have—bells, whistles, rhinestones and electronics.*"

When Helmi talks about the accordion, she has an obvious respect for the instrument, and her family history gives a glimpse at why:

> *The accordion saved my mother's life in World War II. The fact that she could repair, play and entertain made all the difference in her being able to immigrate to the United States.*

Then, founding a successful business, (which led to) my education, and everything that has resulted from the work that I do."

Which also explains why she's not keen on some of the common nicknames for the instrument:

"Belly box" or "squeeze box" is really not giving the appropriate dignity to the technology, the science, the artistry . . . In other countries, the accordion is still treated as seriously as any other concert instrument.

I was already feeling like I was getting in over my head, so I played the only card I had—I mentioned watching Myron Floren on the Welk show. Helmi had a more personal connection to "The Happy Norwegian":

He was my daughter's godfather . . . a great representative of what the accordion can be, and a fine human being.

people who come through here are average accordion players who think themselves extraordinary, because they think, 'I can do everything Myron Floren could do,' which is generally not true.

If a museum filled with hundreds of years of musical history isn't enough, there's the school. The only accordion repair school in the country is here at the museum. It's a nine month curriculum. I didn't ask whether they taught the painting of naked ladies.

Helmi Harrington also teaches privately, and she's had students ranging from a three-year-old to someone who *"only admits to being ninety-one."*

Most of the people I teach are high-tension professionals, and what we do together is meaningful to them not only for relaxing, and entertaining, but also for mental development.

So according to an authority on the subject, accordions help you unwind, make other people happy, and make you smarter. I need an accordion! Or at least, a recommendation of some accordion music I should explore . . .

'Planet Squeezebox'— it's a terrible title, but it's a three CD set that is absolutely wonderful in describing varying ethnic types of accordion music, as well as degrees of seriousness, from the concert stage.

I saved the most important question for last—what does Helmi think of 'Weird' Al Yankovic?

Is he a good accordionist? Not in my humble opinion. But keep in mind that at the museum, we do have his recordings, we do have his picture with the instrument, and I know people who really can't wait to hear what he's gonna do next.

As a side note, and as a public service, I have a recommendation for a place to buy an accordion. While there may be many reputable accordion dealers throughout the country, only one of them used to work out of a converted White Castle, which also happened to be a jewelry store.

Randy McPeck ran Castle Accordion (and Jewelry) in Minneapolis. The place was recently sold, and Randy sells accordions out of his home now, but he was in charge of The Castle for almost two decades.

The building itself has a longer history. It's been moved three times since the thirties, and in the eighties, it was granted landmark historical status, which is why it still looks like a burger joint.

Randy started Castle as a jewelry store, and accordions were just a hobby. Then, his first year, he sold nearly fifty accordions, which led him to realize *"There were more accordion players than I could have ever expected."*

He occasionally had passersby who came in for burgers, and I imagine that presented a challenge. It's hard to upsell someone from onion rings and sliders to musical instruments and jewelry.

Although, he probably did great with the demographic of 'people with disposable income who want to propose marriage in an Italian gondola.'

Randy plays a little of everything from across the accordion map, but *"not anything particularly well."* He considers Eastern European music the most challenging . . .

> *It has crazy time signatures. Most Americans are used to 4/4 or 3/4 time—they can't count out something in 11/16 time.*

I knew that his son played in a band called Paddy and the Buttons, so I asked Randy, who is close to my age, whether young people were picking up the instrument.

> *Yeah, hipsters think they're very cool. Younger people are buying them, but a lot of my customers are people like myself—*

> *We played when we were kids and then when rock 'n roll hit, you learned to hide your accordion. So we put them away, and pick them up thirty, forty years later. I wish I'd never quit playing.*

If someone had never heard accordion music before, wandered in to his shop, and impulsively bought an accordion, they would have a variety of options, from budget to gold-plated.

> *They're still pretty much handmade. The really expensive ones, every single reed is handmade. I've played a $30,000 accordion. It didn't really float my boat all that much. I mean, it was nice . . .*

> *A lot of my customers think they'll play better on a more expensive instrument, thinking it's going to magically make them better. I don't have the heart to tell them they just need to practice. You don't need a new accordion.*

Ultimately, Randy McPeck believes that, rather than a certain type of person being drawn to the accordion, the instrument turns its player into a certain type of person:

> *It's physically demanding – if you have bad technique it can wear you out. Also, accordion players can get pretty fanatical.*

So devotees of the instrument are fanatics, but are they dangerous? Should we be worried about roving gangs of crazed, accordion-toting, Eastern Europeans, terrorizing neighborhoods with their complicated mazurkas? Probably not.

The reality is, the accordion has made a lot of people happy around the world for a couple of centuries. Therefore, I resolve to find a different instrument to mock in my future writings. Piccolo players are just *begging* to be ridiculed.

The Piano Technician

As much as I am impressed by piano players, there's another group that is overlooked by most music fans, yet their contributions to music are as important to what we hear as those of any keyboard virtuoso.

I'm referring to piano *tuners*. They show up hours before any concert or recording session, and their hard work can mean the difference between a great performance and a string of sour notes. Sadly, these people get no applause, and they're never asked to take a bow.

In my own small way, I will attempt to rectify this. I didn't know any piano tuners, but I found a web page for the Piano Technician's Guild. From there, I was able to contact Jim Coleman, Jr., a former president of the PTG. It was time to do what I do best—bother people I don't know.

Since I was an outsider to the world of piano tuning, I tried to get up to speed on the basics. Right away, I learned that 'piano tuner' is not the preferred term, it's piano 'technician,' and I got the sense that 'tuner' is frowned upon. Jim told me, *"We have our own set of jokes, and we spell it 't-o-o-n-e-r.'"*

Okay, so that's not exactly a mic-dropping slam, but at least they have their 'own set of jokes.' I did further research to find some of these alleged 'jokes,' and based on a discussion thread at *pianoworld.com*, they typically involve making fun of people whose pianos are out of tune.

Apparently, some piano technicians pretend they're deaf when they arrive at a site, which probably throws the piano owner for a loop, and must have everyone howling at whatever bars piano technicians frequent.

Another (apparently) often told joke is the following:

> *Piano Technician: I've come to tune your piano.*
>
> *Piano Player: I didn't call a piano tuner.*
>
> *Piano Technician: No, but your neighbors did.*

And here's one you can tell at your next piano tuner party:

> *A tuner named Mr. Opporknockity worked on a grand piano for hours. After he left, an earthquake destroyed the home and damaged the piano.*
>
> *The family called the tuner and begged him to restore their piano, and he refused, saying, "Sometimes, Opporknockity only tunes once."*

I also happened upon a terribly long joke involving two piano technicians, a psychologist, a theologian, and a piano suspended in mid-air, but I would hate to give away the punchline to that one.

Jim Caldwell, my guide to the hidden world of piano repair, has spent over fifty years of his adult life as a professional piano technician. That includes his stint as president of the Guild.

The word 'guild' has always had medieval connotations for me, bringing to mind apothecaries and cobblers with tiny hammers. I asked Jim why the group is called a guild, and he answered, *"Most of us aren't 'union' kind of people."*

It's Jim Caldwell's fifty-fourth year of making a living caring for pianos, and he doesn't seem to be slowing down. Currently, he's responsible for about ninety pianos at the University of Tennessee, in addition to a couple dozen private customers.

Jim is not a performer, and I was surprised to find out that he does not have 'perfect pitch,' that in fact a lot of techs don't have it, and *"I'm sure they're glad for it."*

When you think about it, with all the music we're bombarded with daily, it might be a drag to constantly be aware of whether it's in tune.

Tuning is only a fraction of what a piano technician does--

> *We do all kinds of repairs, rebuilding them, refinishing, moving them, destroying them—that's my favorite part. I've got three in my back yard, waiting for me.*

I was intrigued by the 'destroying' part of the gig. I had not come across that part of the job description in my research. It seems that young Jim got the idea from his dad, Jim Sr., who also was a piano technician.

> *When I was in high school we used to go up into the mountains to service pianos. We would go up into the mining and farming communities.*
>
> *We were driving up these winding roads, and he had heard about a semi load of pianos that went over the edge a number of months before.*
>
> *He was watching out for it, and finally we saw it. We hiked down, and he was just picking up rocks and throwing them at the pianos. To me it was just fun, but I found out later that he was letting go of a lot of stress.*

I can imagine young Jim saying, "Dad? You seem upset-- can I just wait in the car?" Anyway, while Dad was working through his anger issues by throwing stones at Steinways, he was also teaching Jim about pianos.

> *Training takes a lifetime. For years I remember my father coming home, after being in the business for decades, sitting at the supper table, telling my mother, "Well, I learned how to tune pianos today." He'd discovered some nuance to add to our bag of tricks.*

One of those tricks is playing the right piece of music to put the piano through its paces, to make sure it sounds like it should. Different technicians use different music. Jim shared a story about his particular choice:

> *I've been playing the same song for almost fifty years. It's a gospel song entitled "I Am Not Worthy." I tuned this woman's piano, and she was a Christian woman, so she knew the song. She asked how much, and I told her.*
>
> *So she's writing out a check and I'm playing the song. Then she started laughing, and I said "What is so funny?" And she said "Don't you think it's a little weird that I'm writing a check to you while you're playing "I Am Not Worthy"?"*

With pianos being used for so many styles of music, I wondered if his technique or approach changes depending upon how the piano will be used . . .

We like to say we put the same effort into everything, but realistically, if it's for a classical concert, we pay attention to a few more things.

If it's for a rock and roll concert—I've done a few of those where <u>while</u> you're tuning it, they're going "Check check check check." Who gives a hoot? Nobody notices!

It takes the manual dexterity of a surgeon when you're essentially working inside a box filled with a couple hundred thin metal strings.

I've heard of surgeons accidentally leaving things inside patients, but Jim says *"I <u>find</u> more tools than I leave behind."* I asked him some of the surprises he's found.

Mice are somewhat common, and I found a hundred dollar bill once. My dad found the strangest, from my perspective. He had a customer who said her upright piano had a buzz in it.

He checked for the usual things and the buzz wasn't going away. So he pulled the piano away from the wall and looked back in there with the soundboard exposed, and found a .45 revolver.

Apparently, her husband had put it there. Anyway, he put the piano back, began to play, and there was a different sounding buzz now. So, he pulled out the piano again, reached in further, and there was a box of shells!

He handed those to her, confidently pushing the piano back and heard a <u>different</u> buzz. He pulled the other end of the piano away from the wall, and found <u>another</u> .45 and another box of shells, that her husband had apparently 'protected.'

I'm thinking hubby just wasn't very confident in his piano playing, and the firepower was on hand in case his audience got restless. Whatever the reason, this is exactly why there should be a seven-day waiting period and a background check before anyone is allowed to buy a piano.

You might imagine that, with all the technology available today, an old-school trade like piano tuning would have gone the way of lamplighting and phrenology, but Jim had a succinct explanation for why that hasn't been the case.

The real sound of an acoustic piano . . . you can't duplicate it electronically.

Technology certainly helps, though. "*A machine saves me about fifteen minutes per piano.*" As far as Jim's *feelings* about ears and tuning forks versus electronic devices he was guarded. "*There are 'arguments,' yes.*"

Moving on to less controversial subjects, we got back to one of Jim's most unusual customer requests . . .

It was what's called a 'square grand,' from the late 1800s. It's not popular with technicians. I had one delivered sight unseen. The mover said he picked it up in a barn, and the customer said it had been there for twenty years.

It wasn't even all together, it was in pieces. There was a shotgun hole, probably three inches in diameter on one end, and she wanted that saved. It was really firewood, and it was filthy from all kinds of animals, doing everything animals do.

Ignoring the bizarre mental image I had of barn animals getting busy inside a piano, I thought it was interesting that this was the second story that Jim shared which included a firearms component. If I were to list occupations in order of the likelihood of encountering a gun, I would have put 'piano tuner' near the bottom.

Surprisingly, his biggest pet peeve from over fifty years poking around inside pianos has nothing to do with guns.--

It's customers who think they have perfect pitch. You sit at the piano, and they pick out a note and they beat it to death. "You hear that? You hear that?" By the time they're done, it IS out of tune.

I would think an occupational hazard would be uptight piano owners hovering over him while he works, but "*nobody really hovers, and if they do, I ignore them.*"

When I suggested that it might be a bad idea for someone to annoy the person working on their piano, he said, "*Well, there are things we could do.*" It was like a line from *The Godfather,* if the Corleones were a syndicate of piano technicians.

It's good that I had a good rapport with Jim, because otherwise I might be worried. First he's destroying pianos with rocks, then he's 'finding' guns in pianos, and now he sounds like a mobster.

He wouldn't spill the beans on his worst experience with a customer, saying only, "*There's one, whose name I won't mention, who I would never tune for again.*" Overall, he was hesitant to talk about his celebrity clients . . .

I'm not very good about name-dropping. I'll tell you the first famous person I ever tuned for—Ray Charles. I can't imagine how good the tuning was, because that was a long, long, time ago, and I've learned so much since.

It was in Louisville, Kentucky, I was working in a piano factory in southern Indiana, part-time for a dealer in Louisville. They rented a piano for Ray Charles and his group. I didn't get a chance to meet Ray. I stayed till intermission, in case they needed me.

Jim seems content to work without acclaim or even notice, waiting in the wings until he's needed. But the only reason his work isn't noticed is that he's good at it. If you're a piano technician, and didn't do your job well, later that night, a lot of people would notice.

As to my suggestion that the piano *technician* should be brought up onstage after a concerto to take a bow, he was matter-of-fact. *"Well, they should do something. They couldn't do their thing without us."*

The Earworm Savant

Decades before I thought of writing about music, I was afflicted by my first earworm. I blame the Captain and Tennille, although some of the fault lies with the songwriter, Neil Sedaka.

"Love Will Keep Us Together" was the biggest-selling single in 1975. Of course, I didn't have the entire song stuck in my head. In fact, it was only two words, which are repeated four times, at three different points in the song:

I will . . . I will . . . I will . . . I will . . .

That's insidious enough, but then I had the chance to catch the rare and exotic multilingual earworm. I lived in Southern California, and the Spanish-language version was big on the radio. So there I was, walking around with *this* stuck in my head:

Yo soy . . . Yo soy . . . Yo soy . . . Yo soy . . .

I'm as annoyed as anyone when an earworm burrows into my brain, but they've never been more than a nuisance. I'm actually more bothered by the *sound* of the word than the concept. Certain words just inspire queasiness, like 'phlegm,' or 'pustule,' or 'blog.' Or 'queasiness.'

For me, 'earworm' brings to mind unpleasant, squiggly images of horror stories and bugs. I still have disturbing memories of an episode of Rod Serling's *Night Gallery*, and that aired in 1972 (granted, that was an ear*wig*, but it's the same idea).

Earworm is derived from the German '*Ohrwurm*,' which somehow sounds even more unpleasant. According to the Oracle at Wikipedia, it was first used in the 1978 novel *Flyaway*, by Desmond Bagley, but, Wiki being Wiki, it's possible Bagley simply edited his own page to take the credit.

There has probably always been a term for music that pops up out of nowhere. I'm sure there were people in eighteenth century Vienna saying, *"I can NOT get the coda to the second movement of 'Eine Kleine Nachtmusik' out of my head!"*

Sometimes, it's called 'cognitive itch.' In France, they call it 'stubborn music' (*'musique entêtante'*). In Italian, it's 'torturous music" (*'canzone tormentone'*). Oliver Sacks used the phrase, 'sticky music.' I prefer 'tune wedgie.'

Scientists who study these things have more . . . scientific terms. However, I think the most important thing to understand is that *there are scientists who study music!* That would be the perfect gig for me—I would be listening to music for my job, and the research would satisfy my OCD!

Sure, it's not curing cancer, or discovering life on another planet, but if the work of these intrepid scientific explorers can prevent future generations from having the equivalent of an Iggy Azalea tune stuck in their heads, then they're doing God's work.

The Finnish researcher Lassi Likkanen did a groundbreaking study of what he called 'involuntary music imagery (INMI).' The study included a survey of over eleven thousand Finns, the majority of whom just wanted the music in their heads to be *happier.*

At the University of Arkansas, Elizabeth Hellmuth Margulis is director of the Music Cognition Lab, and has written a book called 'On Repeat: How Music Plays The Mind.' She's currently working on a followup, entitled 'On Repeat: How Music Plays The Mind."

I connected with a group of researchers in the U.K., at Goldsmiths, University of London. They're part of a program called *Music, Mind and Brain* (apparently their grant money didn't cover Oxford commas).

As you can see from their picture, they look every bit like the stuffy, dour academics you would expect.

I reached out to Nicolas Farrugia, who at the time was fairly new to the group, to ask a few questions and thereby gain a deeper understanding of the theoretical underpinnings of their research.

I sent an email to Nicolas, and we spoke via Skype. His only restriction was that I make it clear that his work only dealt with the link to brain structure, and that he was not speaking officially on behalf of the Music, Mind and Brain group.

I suppose the group is worried about a grad student going rogue and revealing their secret plans to *weaponize* earworms and place Spice Girls tunes into unsuspecting brains. I didn't pursue that line of questioning. Instead, I asked how the group started.

> *It started because of a BBC Radio 6 show on earworms, where people tell their earworms. (Our) group leader, Lauren Stewart, thought it would be interesting to understand where they come from.*
>
> *She contacted the BBC, and following that, online surveys were setup, and we got a lot of answers thanks to the radio exposure.*

I asked about the musical background of the researchers. Nicolas is from what might be called an *overly* musical family, in that *both* parents were piano teachers. He also took intensive musical training twice a week in violin and percussion starting at age seven.

You might think all that intensity (and practicing) would push a kid as far from music as possible. Remarkably, he seems to have no emotional scars from his childhood, and said the only drawback is that he and his brothers are "*terrible at sports.*"

Nicolas also trained as an electrical engineer in Paris, I guess because it wasn't enough to be a precocious, talented French musician. I'm sure when most people think of the seductive allure of Paris, they think of electrical engineering. Be that as it may, by the time he was twenty-five, he had become primarily a vibraphonist.

Specifically, he was (among other things) a jazz-fusion vibraphonist whose favorite genre is progressive rock. I should have asked him how *that* happens. But then, I started imagining 'Roundabout' played by Lionel Hampton, maybe with a trio, sort of a brushes feel—and I forgot what we were talking about.

His colleagues are an eclectic mix, (classical, jazz, folk, trip-hop), but I was surprised to learn that they usually don't listen to music while working, *"unless there is just myself and the American research assistant."* Sure, blame the American.

Anyway, thousands of people have sent in their earworm stories. Ninety percent of them reported having a tune wedgie at least once a week.

Women, statistically, have more earworms than men, and my *unscientific* explanation is that women, in general, listen better than men. We get earworms, we just don't pay attention to them.

Based on the group's findings, there isn't a single genre that dominates the earworm market. Nicolas gets progressive rock stuck in his head, which is like having other music stuck in your head, except it lasts longer, and there are more synthesizers. And dragons.

Their research has apparently also shown that people have more Christmas songs in their heads around Christmas, which I could have told them, along with a detailed fantasy I harbor involving shopping malls and dead carolers.

Since I was a certified science geek in high school, and I've watched a few episodes of Nova, I should be able to summarize what I learned about the science of music cognition.

> Music something something memory center something long scientific word something hippocampus something something something involuntary something.

Admittedly, I'm oversimplifying.

Basically, there are four triggers for earworms:

Recent Exposure--*The radio just played the Captain and Tennille.*

Mood States—*When I'm under too much stress, I hear the Captain and Tennille.*

Low Attention—*I got bored, and now the Captain and Tennille are in my head.*

Memory Association—*Every time I see my ex, I hear the Captain and Tennille.*

When I asked Nicolas what triggers earworms, he seemed reticent to spill too much, other than to say it *might* have something to do with the intervals between the notes, and repetition.

I think he was being cagey, and that he is using his research to create a super earworm which he will then pitch to Sam Smith who will turn it into a million selling hit.

The most important work being done by *Music, Mind and Brain* is about earworm *removal* (which would also be a great name for a thrashcore band). The results of a survey the group conducted show a range of techniques for removing a particularly stubborn song:

Some people listen to the music that haunts them until the end. Some people try to replace it with another earworm, or sing (the original earworm) out loud.

Tunes that have been used to suppress earworms: 'God Save the Queen', 'Karma Chameleon'" and 'Happy Birthday' . . .

There are some more weird things: some people say that drinking water with a very thin straw can help, and there is a recent paper showing that if you chew gum, you get (earworms) less often . . .

It occurred to me that, since I have already referred to several *potential* earworms in this book, I could be causing my readers unintentional suffering. His response was not very reassuring:

There definitely is a huge risk of contamination. Memory association is a big trigger of earworms.

And it does not even have to be a title, it could just be a single word that makes them think of a tune, or a name of a person that they attach to a tune, or whatever association they can make.

In that case, I apologize for the five songs I've already mentioned in this piece, and the hundred or so other earworms I will have spread by the end of the book. I feel like Patient Zero, infecting people with aggravating songs.

For Nicolas, the most surprising thing to come from all this research has been the discovery that, for some people, earworms actually *help*.

We always talk about the negative aspects, but some people report that earworms help them to focus on a task, or to get things done.

Well, now I feel better. I can tell myself I'm helping people get things done when I bring up "Love Will Keep Us Together." I should stop now, and I will. I will. I will. I will.

The Hippie Philanthropist

The word 'musician' is usually reserved for people who either play, sing, or write music. That seems logical, but on rare occasions, someone's life is so *connected* to music of an era, that at the very least, they should be given the title of 'honorary musician.'

For the counterculture icon known as Wavy Gravy, other titles apply: clown, entertainer, activist, camp counselor. He was even a flavor of ice cream--caramel and cashew Brazil nut ice cream with a chocolate hazelnut fudge swirl & roasted almonds, to be exact. Ice cream gurus Ben and Jerry sold 'Wavy Gravy' from 1993 until 2001.

Depending upon whose account you believe, he also may or may not have prevented thousands of people at Woodstock from taking bad trips on brown acid. He was certainly there, emceeing the festival, but understandably, eyewitness reports about the Sixties haven't always been reliable.

Here's the thing about the history of the nineteen-sixties: truth is usually more meaningful than facts. In the case of Wavy Gravy, the facts are just a tease for the real story. To get the real story, I spoke with the former Hugh Romney about his alter ego.

I wouldn't call our conversation an interview. I prepared a couple dozen questions, but I realized early on that he would be driving the magic bus during our chat. In fact, all I had to do was say that I was calling him from Minnesota, and mention Bob Dylan, and we were off--

> *Actually, I married the 'Girl From the North Country.' (She and Dylan) went to college together, and he almost got her kicked out of her sorority by playing the harmonica when he was just learning. It drove her sorority mates bananas.*

I had the impression that Wavy must have been wired differently from a young age, but he doesn't see it that way . . .

> *That came much later. I guess my big claim of my early existence was when I was five years old. My dad was an architect doing some work in Venezuela, and my mom used to put me out around 9:30, 10 o'clock for my 'morning airing,' and who should come strolling by but Albert Einstein!*

> *He took a fancy to me for some reason, and asked my mother if he could spin me around the block. Her 'flabber' was 'gasted'-- she could barely talk. So, I was set up with Albert. Four or five days a week, for months.*

> *I don't remember much . . . a shock of white hair that predates Don King by half a century, sweatshirt with no logos, sneakers likewise . . . a peculiar smell.*

> *As a youth, you remember odors, and I haven't smelled anything like it since, but someday, I'll walk up to someone and say, "Hey, man—you smell like Albert Einstein!"*

His next 'evolvement' (his word) played out like it does for most of us. It had all the usual elements: Marlene Dietrich, a two hundred fifty year-old sword, and . . . a foot fetish?

> *I attended the theater school at Boston University. They had hired all these amazing teachers that could not work on Broadway because of the McCarthy blackball.*
>
> *I got to study theater with David Preston, and dance with Martha Graham, who I was hot for. She had feet like cypress trees, and I wanted to lick them. I had to restrain myself.*
>
> *They would fly in the great directors of America, and the university got upset because we weren't doing our social studies.*
>
> *So, they were going to move the theater school over to main campus, and the teachers all quit and took me with them to New York, and I ended up with a scholarship at the Neighborhood Playhouse.*

Jazz and poetry may have always shared an audience, but they didn't always share the same venues. It may have happened in California first, but Wavy Gravy created a home for beatniks in New York.

> *I happened to open a Time Magazine, and discovered that they had started 'jazz and poetry' in San Francisco, and I said, "My God, I've written some poems, I know some musicians . . . we can do that!"*
>
> *We set forth in this old basement of a bar on Huntington Avenue called 'The Rock' and the basement was called 'The Pebble in The Rock.'*

We got the Museum School to put in mobiles, paintings, and black tablecloths. It was amazing, and astounding, and that's how I got to start 'jazz and poetry' on the east coast.

So that you don't think I was making up the part about Dietrich and the sword--

I start reading my poems in the coffeehouses in Greenwich Village, ending up at a coffeehouse called The Gaslight.

Downstairs, first, I would just read my poetry. Marlene Dietrich came in and caught my poetry act, and she left a blot of lipstick on her special cup.

The owner, John, who was a crazy man, was very enamored of Marlene Dietrich. He took that cup and put it in a display box on the wall.

The dishwasher came in at three in the morning and said, "Oh, this cup is dirty," and washed it. John chased him down MacDougal with a Revolutionary War saber.

I talked John into allowing folk music to 'occur' in between poems, because it was getting tedious to just do poems. John said, "I made all my money with just poetry," but he tried it, it was great, and eventually, it took over the scene.

In between the poets, I would talk about the weird stuff that happened to me. This guy came by in a suit and said, "Look, just skip the poems, just talk about the weird stuff". Next thing you know, I'm on tour opening for John Coltrane and Thelonious Monk.

When he worked with Monk, Wavy must have had some idea that they were kindred spirits, because their first interaction was a piece of vintage performance art, and Monk played right along:

> *We were playing the Renaissance in L.A., and the dressing room is down a winding stairway at the back of the club.*

> *I came early, with chalk, and I wrote on the steps, 'go back two steps,' and 'spin around three times,' and 'go 'forward nine steps,' and I covered the entire stairs.*
>
> *Then I hid and waited for Monk to show up, and he actually looked at what I had done, and he proceeded to spin around and do the entire stairs, as if I had choreographed him.*

> *He was sweet, like a very sophisticated child. Think of a Paul Klee painting. That was Monk.*

Sometimes, I wish my normal parents had joined a commune and that I had become a hippie, but then I remember that I would have been nine years old at the first Woodstock.

There are plenty of books and movies that deal with the music from the 'Aquarian Exposition,' and I didn't want to throw him questions he's been asked a million times. Still, I couldn't *not* ask Wavy Gravy about Woodstock, so I asked him for some stories we might not have heard.

> *Abbie Hoffman organized the medical services. He separated the doctors from the patients, and set up this huge (medical) tent.*

> *And Chip Monck built the stage at Woodstock. He was also the lighting and sound engineer at the Village Gate, and it was Chip who set up sound and lights for me whenever I performed in the Village.*

Mr. Gravy was much more than an observer at Woodstock. He was the *de facto* head of security. Along with some of his compatriots from their 'Hog Farm' collective, he organized what he called the '*please* force.'

> *The Hog Farm was flown into Woodstock. We had arranged with the promoters to do a free kitchen. When we came off the aircraft, there was the world press saying, "Ah, the Hog Farm! You guys are the security."*
>
> *And I said, "My god, they made us the cops!" The guy said, "Well, yeah." I said, "Well, do you feel secure?"*
>
> *The guy said, "Yeah," and I said, "Well, see, it's working already." He said, "What are you gonna use for crowd control?" and I said, "Cream pies and seltzer bottles."*
>
> *Wes (Pomeroy) was head of the regular police, and he acquiesced to us, and if we ever had real trouble, we would give Wes a shout. Amazingly enough, he later became the chief of police of Berkeley, which is where I live to this day.*

His legal name has been Wavy Gravy for decades, but as exotic as the name seems, its origin is just your basic story involving Job's Daughters, naked water-skiers, and B.B. King.

> *After Woodstock, we returned to our ranch, which resembled a displaced persons camp with a view, because all the hippies on Earth had put their stuff in their cars and come to live with us forever. Oh my God, we felt, "What are we gonna do?"*
>
> *They were having a rock festival in Texas, and there was a rodeo going on, so there was friction. They needed our help, so they actually drove these shiny new buses to our little place in Llano, New Mexico to drive us to Texas.*

We were delighted to get on these buses and get out of Llano, where all these hippies had taken over our scene.

See what happens when hippies move in? This is why we can't have nice things . . .

We were also amazed by the editorial in Time Magazine about our ministrations at Woodstock, and how they were appreciated. And people cheered our buses as we drove through the southwest.

When we got to Texas, we set up camp on Lake Dallas. The concert was at a speedway, maybe six miles away. And we had this beautiful lake, so we were just enjoying that.

Most of the people who came into our Freak-Out tent were not freaking out at all. They were smiling, and sniffing the incense. I actually went on stage and complimented the chemists of Texas for their manufacturing of psychotropics.

So far, everything seems perfectly mellow—enjoying the lake, inhaling some 'incense,' and a tent set up in case anybody freaks out.

Unfortunately, the 'freaking out' didn't come from psychotropically inclined young people, but rather from a fifty-year old, quasi-religious group.

I got woken up at three in the morning by the mayor and the police chief. "The'Job's Daughters' have gone nuts!

They can't handle the skinny-dipping! You showed the world at Woodstock you could police yourselves—you gotta do something!"

> *I said, "Well, if I do something, are you gonna bring a couple truckloads of watermelon for the free kitchen we have set up on Lake Dallas, where we have a free stage?"*

The deal was done. Then it was time for some classic sixties peace-making:

> *I immediately went to the rodeo, and got 'altered' with the rodeo clowns and the bronc riders, and all those guys, and they came and did security for us, and chased away the rednecks. I told the police chief, "I gotta have this boat!"*

> *He immediately gave me the keys to his boat, so I knew he was really nervous. I grabbed a Mae West (life preserver), and I had a bullhorn, and this cowboy hat that used to belong to Tom Mix that had a yarmulke inside, that Lenny Bruce gave me.*

> *We started putting around the lake—"Ahoy! If you wanna stay high, you gotta put your pants on! The Job's Daughters are going nuts! You wanna swim over and tell that other guy, and tell him to tell somebody else?"*

> *Finally, there isn't a bare ass in sight, and the sun is coming out so beautifully. At that moment, there goes a naked water-skier with an enormous erection. I said, "Follow that guy!"*

> *We went around that lake till we ran out of gas, and I made my way back to the free stage and collapsed.*

Understand, I was told by Wavy Gravy's manager that I only had half an hour to ask my questions, and at this point in our conversation, I was worried that I would never hear the story behind his name. Then, I got the real story:

People were going crazy and I hear, "This is mumbly wumbley on mic number 2, come in! How about Wavy Gravy on the floor! Scram, Gravy ain't wavy!"

And everybody's babbling away, and this voice comes over the PA: "BB King is here with his bus. He's gonna play for free—can we clear the stage, please."

I'm getting up real slow, and I feel this hand on my shoulder, and I look up and there is B.B. King.

He looks down at me and says, "Are you Wavy Gravy?" I said, "Yeah, I guess so." And he said "Well, Wavy Gravy, I can work around you."

And he leaned me up against his amplifier, took out his guitar . . . Johnny Winter came from the other side of the stage, they jammed until daytime, and a tiny tip of Texas went to heaven.

For some inexplicable reason, there have been *three* Woodstock festivals, and Wavy was a part of each. His story about the second one indicates that a common denominator between the first two was mud--

They've done three Woodstocks. I've survived them all. The problem that people have is that they keep trying to repeat something, when in reality, each is its own thing.

In Woodstock II, Green Day was on, and they'd just had a great rainstorm, and Billie Joe Armstrong grabs the microphone and says, "I bet you idiots can't hit us with any mud!"

A couple hundred thousand people throwing mud at you—you could plant rutabagas on the stage—the musicians turned brown, they were using mud for guitar picks.

Mike Dirnt was laid out and a security guy is wailing on him, and I said, "Stop! He's the bass player!"

Wavy has kept his positivity flowing since Woodstock, and in 1978, with help from public health experts and spiritual leaders including Ram Dass, he founded the Seva Foundation, with the help of a small grant from a pre-Apple Steve Jobs.

Here again, Wavy's connection to music helped. He got legendary promoter Bill Graham to produce their first fundraiser at the Oakland Coliseum *without Graham knowing it was a benefit.*

The Dead's Bob Weir is on the board, and names like Bonnie Raitt and Dr. John have played shows to raise money for the foundation.

My Sanskrit-savvy readers know that *'seva'* means 'service to humankind,' and it's not just some hippie-dippie slogan. Their focus is eliminating preventable blindness . . .

Eighty percent of the people in the world who are blind don't need to be, and can get their sight back with a fifteen-minute surgery. In thirty-five years, we've helped orchestrate three and a half million sight-saving operations.

Wavy Gravy's other project is Camp Winnarainbow, conveniently located right next to the Hog Farm commune. Kids can learn performing arts, circus skills, and something called 'clown philosophy.' They also run an adult program with the credo, *"It's never too late to have a happy childhood."*

The camp is defined by inclusiveness, and Wavy raises over a hundred thousand dollars a year to make it so that least twenty percent of the children who attend come from economically-challenged families.

I think it's real important that it's not just middle-class and white kids, but the full rainbow.

To wrap up the journey, I wanted come full circle and bring things back to Bob Dylan. I had learned that Wavy Gravy was one of the first people to befriend Dylan in Greenwich Village.

The story was that Dylan wrote the lyrics to "A Hard Rain's Gonna Fall'" on Wavy's typewriter.

I had a room up over The Gaslight that we used to use to get delightfully altered, and create. Bob had an affection for my old Remington, and he blew 'Hard Rain's Gonna Fall' on my typewriter.

Bruce Springsteen was doing the 'Tom Joad' tour, and he says, "You still got that typewriter?" And it was actually eaten by Bekins Movers, along with Lenny Bruce's couch.

They had a fire at a storage facility, and I lost the original draft to 'Hard Rain,' and this amazing velvet couch that Lenny gave me, and a bunch of other stuff. But stuff goes, stuff comes . . .

That is the most concise statement of a personal belief system since Descartes. *Stuff goes, and stuff comes.* We live in a time when acquiring 'stuff' is a guiding principle for some. A credo as simple as *'stuff comes, and stuff goes'* might sound crazy, but it is *definitely* the good kind of crazy.

*I never saw music in terms of men and women,
or black and white.
There was just cool and uncool.*

--Bonnie Raitt

Acknowledgements

All images within are either in the public domain, covered by the Fair Use doctrine, or owned by the author, except:

'Levon Helm' courtesy *parkerjh*

"brain MRI" courtesy *Noran Neurological Clinic*

'John Lennon' courtesy *Roy Kirkwood*

'Quartz Hill Marching Band' and 'Joe Giesler' courtesy *Quartz Hill H. S.*

'Peter Schickele' courtesy *Peter Schickele*

'Vampire Weekend" courtesy *Regan76*

"Mt. Tam" courtesy *A National Acrobat*

"New York skyline" courtesy *King of Hearts*

"Chicago skyline" courtesy *Daniel Schwen*

"Bob Dylan" courtesy *Adrian Lasso*

"Helmi Harrington" *courtesy Accordions Worldwide*

"Castle Accordion' and "Randy McPeck" courtesy *Randy McPeck*

"Music, Mind and Brain" courtesy *"Music, Mind and Brain"*

"Nicolas Farrugia" courtesy *Nicolas Farrugia*

"Miles Davis" courtesy *Peter Buitelaar*

"Jim Caldwell, Jr". courtesy *Jim Caldwell, Jr.*

"Jill Flomenhoft" courtesy *Maceo Paisley*

"Snoop Dogg" courtesy *Jason Persse*

"The Beat" courtesy *Guilherme Tavares*

"Matthew Longbons" courtesy *Matthew Longbons*

"Frank Zappa" courtesy *Helge Øverås*

"Thelonious Monk" courtesy *Ky*

"Bonnie Raitt" courtesy *David Gans*

Printed in Great Britain
by Amazon